CREATIVE
SUPERPOWERS

EDITED BY
LAURA JORDAN BAMBACH / MARK EARLS / DANIELE FIANDACA / SCOTT MORRISON

D1494195

unbound

First published in 2018
This paperback edition first published in 2019

Unbound
6th Floor Mutual House, 70 Conduit Street, London W1S 2GF

www.unbound.com

Text Design by Ellipsis, Glasgow

A CIP record for this book is available from the British Library

ISBN 978-1-78352-903-2 (trade pbk)
ISBN 978-1-78352-552-2 (trade hbk)
ISBN 978-1-78352-554-6 (ebook)
ISBN 978-1-78352-553-9 (limited edition)

Printed in Barcelona by Novoprint

1 3 5 7 9 8 6 4 2

To Dan, Lisa, Sair and Tina.

And to Jon Daniel, our creative Supa Hero. Rest in peace.

CONTENTS

TEACHER

THIEF

INTRODUCTION

Sometimes it feels like every week there's a new emerging technology. It's hard to keep up. Are you feeling a little overwhelmed by all these changes? Is your business agile enough to compete against the new start-ups entering your industry every day? Are you finding it increasingly difficult to connect to your audiences, who constantly stampede from platform to platform? Are you finding it harder to recruit talent who are no longer interested in your business, but instead are magnetised towards businesses with a clear purpose? Are you constantly trying to work out what's next?

These might be some of the things that keep you awake at night. Or the big one: are you worried you might go to work one day to find you've become irrelevant?

You've been replaced. By a robot.

If you've picked up this book, then chances are at least a few of these things are on your mind (unless, of course, you are Elon Musk, in which case you're too busy saving the planet to open this book). As technology continues to open up the world to even more possibilities, it is increasingly hard to keep up.

*

The good news? Our brains are wired to rewire – they can be moulded based on conditioning and behaviour. It's why the hippocampus, the part of the brain that controls conversion from short-term to long-term memory and spatial navigation, is bigger for a London taxi driver than a London bus driver.* While a bus driver drives the same route day after day, a taxi driver has to pull new routes from his or her long-term memory every day. It is this process of reconnecting that stroke victims go through during recovery.

This means that while we feel like we're being left behind, we can also find ways to adapt. Old dogs can learn new tricks, which is amazing, given that we have never had access to such incredible technology. The creative canvas – from 3D printing to virtual reality (VR) to circuit boards and coding devices – has never been so rich. The BBC Microbit, which is making it easy for children to code and unleash their creativity, is a standout example of this.

Technology has also provided brand new routes to market, with the likes of Kickstarter and Indiegogo providing an alternative to the arduous route of venture capitalists, while makers can easily sell their goods on platforms like Etsy. And there is no better example than this book, which has only been published thanks to the support of more than three hundred and fifty people on Unbound (thank you).

If we look at the emergence of artificial intelligence (AI), it's routine jobs that are going to be replaced. Machines are already replacing

---

* Source: http://www.ncbi.nlm.nih.gov/pubmed/17024677

checkout tellers (and Amazon's foray into retail is only going to accelerate that), Uber are trialling autonomous cars, media buyers are being replaced by programmatic buying and a friend who is a metal trader recently told me how hard it's becoming to compete with the robots. However, AI also has the ability to help us rid our existing jobs of some of the routine, which will free up time for us to be more strategic and creative.

Because ultimately creativity is what truly differentiates us from robots. And so, rather than seeing AI as a threat, perhaps we need to look at it from a different perspective, as IA (intelligence augmented). Intelligence augmented is about understanding what computers can do to help unleash our creativity, not just by getting rid of routine, but by giving us information, inspiration and ultimately new connections leading to better ideas. While machines have remarkable capabilities, it is the combination of machine + humans that truly creates magic. This notion of augmented reality is certainly not a new one. Indeed, it was an understanding of intelligence augmented way back in the 1960s that led to the invention of the Mac. Andy Sandoz, CCO at Deloitte Digital, put it nicely at the most recent Kinsale Sharks Awards when he said, 'I'm not worried about technology replacing me, I am waiting for it to release me.'

Thanks to technology, then, we are certain that we are about to enter a new Age of Creativity that will require a new set of creative superheroes to help the world thrive.

*

This book is aimed at making you one of those creative super-heroes by helping you unlock and unleash your nascent creative superpowers.

But before we do, we need to find a way for you to remember what it was like to be a child. So go and find a Lego set and start building off-plan. Remember what it was like to be naturally creative (in the absence of a Lego set, go to YouTube and watch the closing scene of *The Lego Movie* http://ht.ly/nDrw30288z5).

How do you feel? Did it remind you of a time when life did not get in the way and everything was possible? A time when your imagination could run wild and it was easy to picture yourself as a superhero? What was your superpower? Flying at the speed of light, X-ray vision, invisibility, the ability to turn your Brussels sprouts into ice cream?

This book is about unlocking many of the key traits lost since childhood (namely adaptability, curiosity, empathy and fearlessness) as well as unlocking new powers to help you solve your biggest business problems.

We'll uncover the four biggest superpowers that will equip you to thrive in the Age of Creativity:

MAKING – how making opens up new parts of the brain.
HACKING – how becoming a hacker helps you tackle problems
in different ways.

TEACHING – how teaching yourself and others consolidates experience in a fast-paced world.

COPYING – how looking to what already exists helps you solve your problems.

To help bring these four areas to life, we have scoured the globe to bring you stories from some of the creative superheroes who are already solving problems in new and interesting ways. You will hear stories from an architect, a hat maker and a free-noise artist. You will learn how to hack your brain, how to use the street to solve your problems; how to learn from younger generations and how to finish what you started. You will be inspired by how India used hacking to become one of the largest economies in the world, as well as what we can learn from the maker communities of sub-Saharan Africa. And you will be given seven steps for how to make a tool kit for copying from others and some brilliant ideas for building culture in a modern business.

But that's not all.

As David Erixon explains later in the book, the best way to learn is by doing. So we conclude this book with a set of workshops to allow you to hone your new superpowers.

We set out with the aim of writing the most relevant book in the world right now for creative problem solvers across all industries. We cover a wide range of topics across the art and business of creativity. At one end of the spectrum we have Lucas Abela, who details his process as an artist, while, at the other, Annicken R. Day talks about how to build a creative culture in a business. And while at first some chapters might not seem super-relevant to what you are doing right now, you may be surprised by what you can learn from how people in other industries and places are exercising their creative superpowers.

It was also important to us to provide a global view by pulling in authors from India, Japan, Norway, Singapore, South Africa, Sweden, the UK and the USA. And while there is no doubt that many of the authors come from a position of privilege and power, we firmly believe that anyone in the world, in any role or industry, can use some aspects of these creative superpowers to great effect.

As you go through the book, it should also become clear that the creative superpowers are in no way mutually exclusive – you will find notions of hacking, teaching and thieving in Kerry Friend's chapter in the Maker section alone. You will also see some themes evolving which cut across the chapters. These include:

- The importance of the unconscious in the act of creation – that is, the need to allow the brain to make leaps and random associations.
- The need for us to give our brains time to quietly reflect or not think at all.
- The idea of doing and experimenting, rather than passively receiving knowledge.
- The idea of iteration, creativity building on itself.
- The importance of being inspired by those people who are around you.

- The need for you to take responsibility for your own development and learning.
- The importance of being creatively brave and staying true to the butterflies in your tummy.

Finally, it is worth noting that the views of the authors are very much their own, and you will undoubtedly find some things in this book that you disagree with. And that's cool. The important thing for us is that our authors make you think.

So – that's what this book is all about. And we hope that you, too, will become part of a new group of creative superheroes who are going to help build better ideas, better businesses, better societies and a richer, more creative, world. As Construction Guy says to Lord Business in *The Lego Movie*: 'You are the most talented, most interesting and the most extraordinary person in the Universe. And you are capable of amazing things. Because you are the special.'

So, creative superheroes – go make, hack, teach and copy. Let's make everything awesome.

Daniele Fiandaca

Co-founder of Utopia & Creative Social

MAKER

INTRODUCTION

By Laura Jordan Bambach,
Creative Partner at Mr President

From recording a seminal eighties track, to painting a watercolour, to finishing writing this chapter, the creative process that is making can be plagued with errors, dead ends and moments of seemingly insurmountable stuckness.

But by making, committing notes to tape or pen to paper, you begin a process of creative alchemy that can also spark invention and end in great feats of creative genius. Making is both the creative process and the method by which significant leaps across culture are made. It's both the means and the end. Without making, ideas stay just that, progress grinds to a halt and we all resign ourselves to the rise of the robots as we sit about and cogitate. It's enough to give you a serious case of the Morlocks.*

Making is the magic and the flow, the grind and the grease to the wheel. It can be laser-focused on a goal or more exploratory,

---

* In H. G. Wells's novel *The Time Machine*, humans of the future are divided into two distinct species: the Eloi – beautiful, fragile creatures who have lost the ability to create anything for themselves and have to be provided for completely; and the Morlocks – the clever, inventive and thoroughly disgusting race that controls them from their underground lair.

feeling and probing for the right answer. There's no right way to make other than to just get started. To start anywhere, and eventually, to finish. To learn from the successes and failures, and to start again. Because everything needs to be made in order to be made real, and the making process defines every articulation of every creative vision.

The very errors, dead ends and stuckness that rub against us and frustrate our delivery of great work are in fact the creative opportunities that lift us above the robots and define the peak of human creativity. The yin to the 'Eureka!' moment's yang. Machines can indeed do the work, but progression and innovation depends on the imperfections of the human creative process, on making.

In some way, everyone thinks of themselves as a maker (everyone creates something, right?), but making is more than just seeing an idea through to completion. To make (rather than just 'do') is the process of exploring new concepts and ideas through tangible experimentation. The testing out of ideas through the process of actually making it, rather than going from start to finish in a staid, linear fashion with no room for changes.

So, what is it to really embrace the practice of making? And why is it so important, beyond the fact that you, well, get stuff . . . made? Why is it one of our four key creative superpowers?

Because, despite what we've become accustomed to seeing as 'real', nothing happens without making; everything else is just conjecture.

As the old economists' joke goes: 'it works in practice, but what about in theory?'

In this section we hear from four of the most talented and passionate makers in their fields from around the world, in order to understand their personal theories of making, and how to apply those theories to your own work and life.

What you get out of it will very much depend on what you make of the wisdom of their experiences. In the next four sections, I'll introduce our makers and the key theories they uncover.

MAKING IS THE CORE OF CREATIVITY

Alice laughed: 'There's no use trying,' she said; 'one can't believe impossible things.'

'I daresay you haven't had much practice,' said the Queen. 'When I was younger, I always did it for half an hour a day. Why, sometimes I've believed as many as six impossible things before breakfast.'

– Lewis Carroll, *Alice in Wonderland*

Let's take a moment to look under the hood of the creative process, which looks more or less the same whether you're writing a hit single, a book or a line of code.

There's little magic to it; it's a well-documented series of steps to help you hit your creative peak. Trust in the process (and fill your creative bank enough upfront) and ideas will flow. Here's how it usually goes:

1. Feed your brain with as many divergent ideas as possible. Reach far and wide for inspiration. Be interested, and interesting.
2. Discuss and explore these ideas in new ways, on your own and with others. Collaborate, share thoughts.
3. Give your subconscious enough time to process and connect the dots. Dream, take a bath, distract yourself.
4. Eureka! The spark of an idea is born.
5. Find your 'flow' and get busy making your idea come to life.
6. Repeat.

This simple approach to solving a creative problem works, but there's another way to apply your creativity to a problem – one where ideas are discovered through the process of making itself, and it's not just your subconscious but your hands that are connecting the dots.

The standard, mechanical process for getting to an idea can be likened to architecture, where a form is built from the ground up, organised and planned every step of the way, with a clear goal established. But the more explorative creative process is more like sculpture, where small pieces of stone are chiselled away to reveal the image underneath, the form changing and adapting to the materials and the environment in real time. There's a vision of where it's headed, but not necessarily a fixed goal or a reliable plan. And there are some incredible creative folk who embrace this different way of working.

Morihiro Harano is one of the world's most respected and award-winning creative minds, as well as one of its most humble and generous voices. Responsible for consistently incredible work, both exquisitely crafted and strategically sound, his Tokyo studio, Mori Inc., is small, nimble and formidably talented. He's worked for everyone from Honda and NTTDocomo to OK Go, the band famous globally for their synchronised music videos.

In fact, it's Mori's work with OK Go that really drives home the power of making. His music video for the song 'I Won't Let You Down' is one long take – over five minutes of incredible synchronisation on a scale difficult to comprehend, and with a cast of hundreds. Yet, rather than planning and storyboarding the video in its entirety before filming, then hiring an expensive studio where mistakes are discouraged, Mori and the band cheaply hired an unoccupied shopping mall and allowed the playful process of making to unfold in order to 'discover' the details of the piece together.

In this case, director and artists work as one, stepping on each other's toes and playing in the 'sandpit' of the task at hand. Over a number of weeks, ideas for the video unfolded and were refined through doing. Think of it as a kind of creative prototyping, using the evolutionary power of making to get to a wonderful final output through experimentation. By working through concepts as they went, the 'dance' that Mori captured in his final shot was born, astonishingly perfect.

Mori's chapter, 'What Makes for Great Making?', is a window into the world of one of the best contemporary makers. The process he shares can be applied to any creative task to improve the quality of your work, and the enjoyment you take from it.

MAKING HAS A CONSCIENCE

We are the music-makers,
And we are the dreamers of dreams,
Wandering by lone sea-breakers,
And sitting by desolate streams.
World-losers and world-forsakers,
Upon whom the pale moon gleams;
Yet we are the movers and shakers,
Of the world for ever, it seems.

– Arthur O'Shaughnessy, excerpt from *Ode*

'We are the music-makers'. One of the most sampled poems of all time, appearing everywhere from Gene Wilder's Willy Wonka to the electronic music of The Aphex Twin and 808 State. But why has this poem resonated so powerfully with creative folk, long after Arthur O'Shaughnessy himself has faded into relative obscurity?

When he penned those words in 1873, O'Shaughnessy was describing creators themselves, those of us with the ability to set the vision of the world for others to follow. The makers – artists, musicians and philosophers on whose creations new things are built, and progress is made. Those makers whose dangerous and radically new creations move the world forward.

We are all free to have these dangerous ideas, to explore and conduct our own thought experiments. Our minds are wondrous, and part of the creative process is to challenge yourself to think the unthinkable. But when you set to making something, to form one of these dangerous ideas into something tangible, it takes on a power it didn't possess as thought alone.

There is a certain energy born out of making something new which is powerful enough to fire the imaginations and bend the ears of a large group of people. That's some potent stuff, and a big responsibility. So creativity has long been associated with doing incredible good. Of making a conscious choice to 'be the change we want to see in the world' (thanks, Gandhi).

Kerry Friend is deeply involved in the maker communities of sub-Saharan Africa. A digital advertising and design superstar in her native South Africa, she's famous for tackling a brief with incredible creativity, and has a passion for solving problems and driving change. In fact, her whole maker network is built around doing the most good through creativity. From new tools to recycle and extrude plastics as base materials for projects, to the emphasis on education and supporting poorer communities, every part of the maker network is committed to not only making, but making the world better, too.

*

In her essay Kerry tours many of these maker spaces to speak with the incredible entrepreneurs behind them, and finds many irons in the fire, many projects, many spaces, but one goal – a better Africa built in part by creative work.

MAKING IS EVOLUTIONARY

Everything one does in one's life forms the building blocks for the next big thing to explore. As a maker, everything you *have* done influences everything you do in the future – mistakes made and corrected, skills learned, themes refined, new threads of opportunity discovered. The next idea is a natural evolution from the last thing you've made.

In technology this 'agile' approach is mainstream. As the Facebook mantra goes: 'fail fast', and we come across MVP in the start-up world continually. Agile is just another word for iterative making, so why is it so popular in these fields? Because you can be first to market with an idea, because you can be more nimble and responsive and because you put the people most responsible for the success of the project front and centre: your audience. There's a lot to be learned from agile methodology which can be applied to any creative journey.

But what technology has renamed 'test-and-learn strategy' has been a mainstay of the creative process since day dot. Evolution and progression of one's ideas, and skill set, happen through the process of making something.

*

Lucas Abela is an Australian free-noise artist, whose phenomenal story lays bare his creative process and constant development, from the moment a freak accident (and subsequent wiring mistakes) created the musical inspiration that altered the course of his creative career.

Over the course of twenty-five years, his performances have evolved into an ever more complex spectacle, with every evolution being more epic and inviting more audience participation. His piece is a journey from experimentation and apparent chaos to complex and highly evocative work through the constant evolution of projects and a passion and curiosity for making.

MAKING IS PROLIFIC

William Burroughs, Brion Gysin, Björk, David Bowie, Kathy Acker . . . they have all fuelled their creativity through the process of making. In fact, whether it's using cut-up techniques to inspire new ideas or repeating the same imagery or process over and over again to get to a heightened creative state, there's a lot that can be learned by applying these techniques to other creative problem solving.

And the more diverse the starting points the more interesting the output, as concepts are mashed together in the making.

Lizi Hamer is a creative director based in Singapore who is passionate about where ideas come from in the first place, and how having a making practice can help to develop ideas in new and interesting ways.

These techniques can unblock your creative impasse. They can inspire fresh thinking and help you to unlearn old solutions that are no longer useful. They can encourage you to see the right idea among the wrong ones, and help you find your creative flow.

In her piece, Lizi looks at how the prolific process of making can achieve all this, and the importance of a spare parts pile of ideas and inspiration to draw upon.

Across the four pieces in this chapter, you'll discover the importance of making as the core creative driver for innovation and creative excellence, allowing you to step into the bodies of four of the most prolific and interesting contemporary makers from around the world. With our expert makers from noise art, to experiences, films and creative technology – there are four incredible minds presented here with which to meld. We encourage you all to be lateral *tinkers*, not just lateral thinkers, in order to make the most of your creativity.

WHAT MAKES FOR GREAT MAKING?

By Morihiro Harano,
Creative Director/Founder of Mori Inc.

People often say my work is unique, and are curious about my methods and making process. Although I try to answer their questions as best as I can, creativity is something that is difficult to subject to logical, linear analysis. So, I would like to take a less formal approach, and pretend for a few minutes that we are sitting around a table, talking and sharing a bottle of Japanese *sake*. Let me share my thoughts with you on how to create the right conditions for making the extraordinary.

1. DON'T STUFF YOUR HEAD WITH TOO MANY FACTS

An abundance of knowledge does not produce an abundance of creativity. In fact, I believe the opposite is true. Stuffing your head with too many facts can seriously degrade the quality of your creative work.

To many people this is counter-intuitive. They believe the answer to any business problem can be found by thoroughly studying the issue, the market research and the audience. Such an approach may be fine if your only goal is to keep the status quo or solve a simple dilemma. But if you want to set your sights higher, initiate change and impress with truly outstanding work, you should limit your information intake.

Why? Because the more you know about something, the more you limit your creative freedom. Each additional fact becomes a checkpoint to be cleared. If you design your solution to clear all of the checkpoints, it will be just like any other solution that clears all the checkpoints. In this context, knowledge is the enemy of creativity. To truly exercise your creative imagination, you need to discard ideas that have previously been held sacred.

Uber is a good example. Uber's business model is highly creative, and has become a worldwide phenomenon. But it was not the brainchild of someone with long experience in the taxi business – it was created by people who ignored all the conventions of the taxi industry and came up with a service that no one had thought of before.

At school we are taught that knowledge and learning are essential to success. But if you want to create something that is truly 'new', too much knowledge can get in the way. Rather than poring endlessly over the context, brief or market data, listen closely to what people say, and pay attention to the words that resonate in your heart. When inspiration strikes, trust your instincts.

2. DON'T DIVE IN ALONE

Before you begin a project, remember that two heads are better than one. Don't dive right in thinking about *how* to proceed.

Stop and think about *who* you want to work with. Who are the people you need to help you succeed? Find them, and get them involved.

I find that with a few rare exceptions most people are more creative and productive when they are thinking and working with others as part of a team. As a result, I like to take a 'sandbox' approach to creativity.

Let me explain. If you watch children playing in a sandbox, you can see multiple innovations being made in a very short time. Each child may start out on its own, doing its own thing. But if one child builds a cool-looking mountain, the others will start building cool-looking mountains, too. And if one digs a hole in the side of a mountain, another will dig in from the opposite side. Behold! A tunnel is born. Learning and interacting in a group, the children stimulate each other to make new discoveries.

Sandbox-style creative development works for me. I assemble a team – including people with widely different areas of expertise if I can – and we all play with ideas as a group.

My company, Mori Inc., consists of only three people: a creative director (me) and two assistants. Although most ad production companies have at least one copywriter and art director on staff, I prefer to keep in-house personnel to a minimum, effectively enforcing my use of sandbox-style creative development. Depending on the project, I may work with industrial designers, choreographers, composers, or programmers. People in these fields are already often involved in production work, of course, but usually not at the very beginning – in the sandbox – when initial creative ideas are developed. With a more conventional approach, the copywriter and art director are the only kids in the sandbox.

To sum up: don't depend only on your own ideas. Brainstorm with other people. Not always the same people, but, rather, a group you don't usually work with. Because to create something new, the creative process itself must be new. It is the process – not the project – that is most important. Create the process, and the project will take care of itself.

3. INVADE EACH OTHER'S TURF

I find that a group of people who have very different talents can generate truly original ideas quite quickly. But for such a group to work effectively, everyone must agree to one rule: it's OK to invade each other's turf.

Creative professionals tend to be very circumspect when commenting on another creative professional's work. It's as if there is an unwritten rule that we must respect boundaries; that we are out of line if we comment on a subject outside our own area of expertise. I find this kind of thinking to be very detrimental to the creative process. It is only when everyone agrees to speak freely, and listen objectively, that true creativity can be achieved.

I think copywriters can contribute to design, creative directors to film editing and designers to a musical soundtrack. Truly gifted creators are open to new ideas, wherever they come from, and use those ideas to create something even better.

A music video I made for the band OK Go provides an example here. OK Go is famous for its quirky videos, most of which are shot in a single take. But in rehearsal for this video, we discovered we had a serious problem. To shoot the video in one take as planned, there was a point at which there was simply not enough time to move the camera from position A to position B. We tried to overcome this problem in all kinds of ways, but none of them worked. We were truly stuck.

So I suggested the unthinkable: rewrite the song to give us enough time to move the camera. The point at which we needed to move the camera fell right at the bridge, which was four measures long. I suggested doubling the length of the bridge to eight measures, which would give us the time we needed to move the camera.

When my suggestion was conveyed to the band members, an awkward silence fell over the assembled crew. For someone from the video production side to suggest to an artist that the music should be rewritten was unheard of.

But the band's reaction was 'What a great idea!' And they extended the bridge on the spot to allow us to get the shot in one take. The resulting video, 'I Won't Let You Down', went viral faster than any other OK Go music video to date.

I believe this willingness to accept the suggestions of non-experts – to let them invade your turf – is vital to the creative process. As I said earlier, knowing too much about a subject can restrict your creative vision. Whatever your area of expertise, it's important to remain open to suggestions from any quarter.

4. THROW STUFF AWAY

To create something new, you must get rid of the old. This is a truism that is difficult to deny. And when you lead a creative team, it is sometimes necessary to be heartless in your judgements, and discard ideas that team members have worked very hard to create.

The need for personal validation is human nature. But if you cater to that need, it can be very detrimental to the creative process.

'Xylophone in the Forest' is one of my best-known works, and provides a good example of what I'm talking about. For this project, we constructed a wooden xylophone 44 metres long on a forested hillside. It was designed so that a wooden ball placed at the top would roll down the entire length, striking each of the xylophone's bars (over 400 in all), playing a melody from one of Bach's most famous compositions.

The media artists in charge of constructing the xylophone didn't really like the idea of a long, straight xylophone. They thought it would be more interesting to create a sort of Rube Goldberg machine. Although my original idea was for a long, straight xylophone, I followed the 'It's OK to invade each other's turf' rule and agreed to the construction of an alternative, Goldberg-like device.

*

Constructing the two types of xylophone took over three months, most of which was spent creating the Rube Goldberg version. We then set each xylophone up in the forest and filmed the action. Because it was their own idea, the xylophone production team naturally liked the Rube Goldberg version better.

But after editing both films and screening them, I disagreed. Although the complicated machinery of the Rube Goldberg version was interesting to watch, I felt the purity and simplicity of the straight-line version was much more effective. When I told the team my decision, they were understandably downcast and fought hard to get me to change my mind. After all, the Rube Goldberg version had been far more difficult to build, and to have it rejected by a creative director who hadn't witnessed all the labour that went into it was naturally very painful to them.

But if I had agreed with them, I do not think that 'Xylophone in the Forest' would have received the accolades that it has. Although rejecting the Rube Goldberg version was a painful decision to make, subsequent events have made it clear that it was the correct decision. And today, sharing in the global acclaim that the project has earned, the people who built the xylophone give it pride of place in their portfolio.

5. SLEEP!

A lot of people think that working long hours is a good thing. But when it comes to creative work – particularly in the early stages, when you're trying to come up with ideas – I believe working long hours is a very bad idea.

When I tell some people this, they get angry. 'What's wrong with working all night? Are you crazy? All-nighters are a fact of life!'

I beg to disagree. Because when I think of an idea, it is not 'me' that thinks of it: it is my brain. 'I think, therefore I am', as Descartes famously said. It is the brain – a living organism – that is the source of ideation, not the self. The self only exists within the confines of the world our brains allow us to perceive.

Our brains are far more active than we realise. This is demonstrated by a phenomenon known as the 'cocktail party effect', which refers to the brain's ability to filter out the background chatter when we are in a crowded room, and selectively bring to our attention only information that is relevant – such as when someone across the room mentions our name.

Ideation is often described as the process of combining two pre-existing concepts to form a third, new, concept. But little is understood about the inspiration that triggers this process. Scientists do know that to conceive new ideas a person must begin with a certain baseline level of information. They also know that new ideas are more likely to emerge when the person is in a relaxed state. But why is this so?

I believe it is because ideas are not created by the self, but by the brain, working outside of our consciousness.

*

When we sleep, our brains continue to perform tasks like organising short- and long-term memories, which in turn can appear to us in the form of dreams. I believe this is where ideas are born, with our dreams as we sleep.

But because ideas are born outside of our consciousness, they are not immediately available to us. Although they exist within our brains, we are not yet aware of them. And as soon as we wake up in the morning, our brains have to go to work again. That's why it's important to set aside time for contemplative reflection, relieving stress on the brain so that it can reveal those ideas to us in a moment of inspiration. It is also why many books about the creative process emphasise the importance of a quiet and relaxing workplace, and why many people say they get their best ideas when they are taking a bath or engaging in some other low-stress activity.

I believe there are three things our brain needs in order to produce ideas: 1) a baseline level of knowledge about a subject or project; 2) sleep, so our brain can process new information and concepts into ideas; and 3) time and space for quiet reflection after we get up, so we can reduce the load on our brain to allow it to communicate those ideas to our conscious mind.

Like much of neuroscience, this is just a theory. But by putting this theory into practice, I have arrived where I am today. The theory's validity is also borne out at the many companies around the world that have created more relaxed, low-stress working environments.

They don't do it because it looks cool; they do it because it actually helps people be more creative.

The point is this. Show a little respect for your brain – it is where all your ideas originate. Take care of it, and try to ease its stress load.

Lots of people keep physically fit by dieting or working out. But in creative professions, mental fitness is equally important. If you want your creative work to stand out, get some sleep.

6. DON'T MAKE SHIT FOR SHIT

First of all, let me apologise for my crude language. The subject I want to talk about is honesty.

I've been working in the creative industries for over twenty years, and I've been to many client briefings for products that were, to be honest, total shit. (Sorry!) But the agency or design studio staff would usually say, 'Wow, what cool shit!' And the client would be pleased and we would all go off and make another shitty ad. And then we would go to the South of France to give awards to each other for making the best shit.

Why did we do it? The answer, of course, is money. People paid us money to make shit for shit. This is not a problem limited to the advertising industry. Manufacturing companies, for example, also suffer from it.

*

I think it's time to put an end to such nonsense. From a global perspective, it's a waste of creative talent and resources.

Clients, ad agencies and design companies are all makers in their own right. So why don't we all gather around a sandbox, speak honestly and work together to create things in a new way? If we can loosen our grip on knowledge-based preconceptions and agree to think as a team, remaining open to suggestions but willing to let go when necessary, I think we will be able to produce much, much better work.

To make this happen, though, total honesty must be held as the highest virtue. Whether you're the client, the agency guy, or the designer, when the situation calls for it, you've got to be able to say, 'this is shit'. You've also got to be able to keep your cool if someone says that about your work, and think only about how to move forward.

Creators should always be brutally honest. Caring too much about social niceties and the feelings of others is a sure way to disrupt the creative process.

7. LOVE AND RESPECT

Finally, I want to talk about setting creative goals, and the characteristics that define truly great work.

Whether we're talking about brands, products, fine art or entertainment, there are two things common to work that move people deeply: love and respect. To be loved and to be respected – these are natural human desires that resonate with, and motivate, people around the world.

I believe that human beings are programmed to value love and respect at a very fundamental level. In fact, I believe our survival as a species owes much to the love and respect that motivates us.

As biological organisms, human beings are notably ill-equipped for survival. We don't have the fangs of a lion or the speed of an antelope. The only reason we have been able to survive and flourish to the point of becoming the planet's dominant species is because we are bound together by love, and excel at organising ourselves into strong social groups.

Most social groups, whether they are families, countries, freegan movements, or brand loyalists, are united by a shared love. We are programmed to empathise with others who love the same things, and it is these bonds of empathy that have enabled us to endure.

Of course, the ability to form groups is not, by itself, enough to ensure survival. Leadership is also required. And leaders can only lead when they are respected by others. Consider creative luminaries like Steve Jobs, The Beatles, Stanley Kubrick and Banksy. We honour them because they have earned our love and respect.

The human need for love and respect is primal, but it is of a higher order than the need for food or sex. It has a near-universal power to inspire. And whether we work in advertising, branding, product design, fine art, or entertainment, if we want to produce great work it must be the quest for love and respect that guides our evolution.

———

These are my observations on the creative process. Like the process itself, they are fluid and constantly evolving, driven by an impulse that cannot be defined with logic or language. Ethereal and shape-shifting, it is the creative impulse that lurks in the spaces between words and actions, providing a tantalising glimpse of the next great idea.

MAKER CULTURE IN SOUTH AFRICA

By Kerry Friend, Creative Director at Bear Season

THE MAKERTHON YEARS

I grew up in a farming town – no, wait, just *outside* a farming town – in South Africa. Don't panic: I won't be regaling you with long childhood stories about the times I built forts in the bushveld and under bridges next to the railway tracks. Or that time I built a plywood box at the bottom of the garden, which I insisted on 'living' in. And I won't go into detail about the 'robot' necklaces I used to make using nuts and bolts, and a big marble for its eye, all held together with Prestic, which I proudly strung around my neck on a piece of string.

But as TV- and computer-starved children we had to resort to willing our imagination into being using odds and ends found in the dusty garage and, of course, at least one shiny thing from mom's cupboard. And it wasn't until some thirty-eight years later that I realised how incredibly lucky I was to live in that single main road town, with long afternoons spent wandering around the bushveld bored out of my mind.

*

Because that mix of boredom and having to entertain myself for hours on end made me a natural and accomplished maker. I was having long sessions of focused making, 'makerthons', for hours, days, months . . . In fact it was about an eleven-year-long maker-thon, before I became a Madonna/Morrissey wannabe (yes, in one outfit) and left my childhood maker years behind me.

MAKING IT AS A CREATIVE PROFESSIONAL

Those makerthon years contributed to my imagination running away with itself with some regularity. I had a brief run-in with compulsive lying, but that's another story. As a result I was able to land a job in advertising. 'As a result of makerthons, or briefly being a compulsive liar?' I hear you ask. Probably both. I was able to play with ideas and make them come to life. But when I made the move into digital I simultaneously rekindled my love of analogue and physical objects. All connected to digital, of course, because high-touch experiences and physical participation is what people still enjoy and are delighted by. The mix of the two is magic.

So my maker mindset really resurfaced when I started working in digital communications. This was evidenced in my work, as I was always trying to inject some physical object or experience into my creative projects. For example, when I was at hellocomputer we turned the Johannesburg Zoo's honey badger into their social media spokesanimal by using infrared motion sensor technology to connect its physical movements to Twitter. In fact, every creative in my team knew they had to bring me work which bridged the physical and digital world. (Sigh. Poor guys.) So this whole element of playing and making really did set me up to think of objects (physical or digital) as tools to be used in creative ways and not necessarily for what they were intended.

I was so enamoured with the idea of playing and making just to see what happens that I approached my then exec. creative director, Brett Morris (now CEO of FCB Africa Group), who was incredibly generous in allowing me, and at times funding, these experimental makerthon sessions. (Most important was the twenty-four-hour coffee supply.)

These makerthons really brought playing and making into agency life, and there were a few projects that were carried through and developed into bigger projects. But the entire focus of my version of a hackathon or makerthon was for creatives, thinkers and developers who worked in groups together – almost simulating a mini agency – to let go of the idea of an end goal or formal brief and just play within a very broad theme to see what happens, e.g. hack for music, hack for kids, hack for holidays.

My maker mindset has really informed how I approach creative projects and has made my thinking a lot more nuanced, human and fun.

MAKING A DIFFERENCE

After a while I became quite involved in the maker and hacker community. I met makers from all different backgrounds, all of whom had their own particular skills that they applied to the maker process – engineers, artists, industrial designers, teachers and people who believed in the difference a maker culture could make to people's lives and in turn livelihoods.

This realisation opened up a whole new world for me and showed me how a maker culture could have a higher social purpose; in a country where the education system was failing children, for instance, it could actually have a massive social impact. Maker culture was also being used to develop a start-up community to help with job creation and to mobilise a wave of entrepreneurship.

So my personal maker experience is just a very small facet of a very healthy maker culture that is developing in South Africa, and in this chapter I wanted to include the voices of some of the makers and hackers I have met along the way. This community is full of good people going above and beyond to make spaces, sometimes in their own homes, for people to play and create.

What follows, then, is a series of contributions from these awesome, spirited people, who offer their thoughts on why they're passionate about making, and how it's making a positive change in South Africa. In their own free-flowing words.

TIYIANI NGHONYAMA COO of Geekulcha, and Librarian of Maker Library Network South Africa, sponsored by The British Council

The Geekulcha Student Society (GKSS) was first established at the Sol Plaatje University in Kimberley, Northern Cape Province, in

2015. GKSS (http://geekulcha.com/) seeks to grow a Geek Culture on campus to stimulate, cultivate and accelerate Student Innovation: where the YOUNG, TALENTED, SKILLED, CREATIVE and AMBITIOUS tech minds meet to LEARN, CONNECT with industry leaders, get EXPOSURE & put their SKILLS to WORK.

While building a geek culture through Geekulcha with over 9,000 students in South Africa, the biggest lesson I've learned is that you need to build and keep a very vibrant community. A lot of the makers want a sense of belonging and being involved in this digital-smart growing world. I am a firm believer that these three things go together: **Tools, Process and People.**

More often than not, many tend to present tools to the people and expect them to make magic. This method has been failing and will exhaust the spirit of making and makers. A culture has to be instilled, an ecosystem must be created and given the necessary support.

Maker education also needs an established, sustainable model as opposed to small one-off events where people get to make cool objects, but then there is no follow-through beyond that event to turn that experience into something of value for that person or community.

If local government and investors helped build a sustainable ecosystem with the correct support structures in place, for example project management skills and financial support, some of these fun projects could be taken further and realised, and could then contribute to socio-economic growth in South Africa where over half of the youth population is unemployed.

MARC NICOLSON Thingking Studio and Librarian of Maker Library Network South Africa, sponsored by The British Council

To me the part about making that I connect most with at the moment is fixing. To fix something is probably a combination of making and copying.

To be fixed, an object needs to be understood. Fixing should be more than sticking something back together. The question 'how and why did it break?' should be asked. The fix should then make it not only usable again, but more robust than before. The value of this approach will help all people understand the physical world better, including materials, processes and design. This will then enable the making of new things that will not break as easily.

Fixing for me can also include putting two or more objects together to make something new. A big part of the maker movement also needs to be documentation. Instructables for me is one of the most powerful ideas – a forum for putting ideas out there and getting others to make suggestions to improve on them. In South Africa the ideal outcome of fixing and then making is the possibility of sharing unique skills and solutions with locally found materials and the passing on of this knowledge to other areas with similar materials.

MIA VAN ZYL South African designer–maker

To me, making, learning to make or teaching someone else to make something for the first time transports you to a place or moment where you believe ANYTHING is possible: 'If I'm able to make this thing I knew nothing about just a while ago, or try out this technique I've never tried before, WHAT ELSE IS POSSIBLE?'

When we plan or get together as members of the South African 'maker family' for a collaborative event or meet-up, the craziest, most amazing (and often most hare-brained) conversations happen while our hands are busy and our senses engaged – your brain starts connecting dots in a totally different way than, say, when you're busy doing a known task by yourself. 'What if this was possible?' 'Let's try it!' 'Why not?'

For those engaging in a collaborative making workshop for the first time, having your hands busy and your mind engaged in this 'different mode' can facilitate stimulating conversations that would never happen otherwise. Just knowing that it's OK not to know, that the point is experimenting and sharing and playing without fear of failure (whether you try once or ten times!), can be quite an impactful experience, or at the very least FUN. It could be exactly those types of conversations (even the hare-brained ones!) that set the ball rolling on an innovative solution or provides a fresh angle on an old issue.

There are myriad ways to engage with making on any and every level: some people love to tinker, learn and try out new processes, techniques or materials all the time, finding enjoyment in the process itself and never actually making an end product – I call these 'process makers'. Other people are keen on trying out something new as a challenge to master and enjoy having something physical to show for it; yet others are intent on solving a specific problem and find the shared resources, know-how and participatory nature of maker spaces an enjoyable environment in which to dream and scheme, design, prototype, iterate, ask for and share advice, and create a final product – they're what I call 'product makers'.

I believe that while so much of our lives are led in the digital realm and happen on touch screens, as sensory beings many of us yearn for a tactile experience – to have something in our hands that we can physically transform by touch and feel – whether it's kneading dough, carving wood, building an Arduino kit, learning to solder or creating something new from a mix of upcycled curiosities. Or participating and experiencing how you bring something imagined and modelled on screen to life as a 3D printed artefact.

The best part for me? Being part of an enriching, sharing and imaginative 'family' where anything and everything is possible – as long as you're willing to get in there and try.

STEVE GRAY The maker space in Durban

Hacking-machines are a combination of components working together towards one function. In most cases it's easier to adapt an existing machine to perform a different function that to figuratively 'reinvent the wheel'. Hacking is about finding the most convenient, economical or fastest workable solution, which by definition is not perfect for the new task, but a good hack means that it's good enough.

My best example would be the time I used a 30kg CNC router as a 'selfie stick' while travelling. Sometimes it's as simple as using hairspray as build plate adhesive for a 3D printer, or some cable ties and a spoon as a replacement for a cupboard handle.

Making – the term has grown to mean more than just putting things together. It encapsulates the ethos of the open-source movement, where sharing skills and designs is the norm. You no longer need to be an inventor to make something; now it can be as easy as watching a YouTube video and teaching yourself how to make furniture from old water bottles, or building a complex robot to automate an assembly line.

My best experience so far is making a DLP (UV light-curing) 3D printer by following designs and instructions from a project on the internet. It really is mind-blowing to be wearing a wedding ring made for my first 3D print off this machine, the entire cost being less than my original white gold ring. I've also built spray-painting robots like Jürg Lehni's Hektor that didn't work, mainly because designs were not very well documented and I lost interest after getting stuck for too long.

TOM VAN DEN BON Binary space

Long before making was a thing, South Africans were doing it. *Oupa* (grandfather) was tinkering in his car and *Ouma* (grandmother) was busy in the kitchen canning peaches and baking 'koeksisters'. I think the urge to make or modify has always been strong. Probably because of our location, goods weren't easily or cheaply obtained and sometimes you had to make it work (hack it!).

Fast-forward many years to today, and we still have that urge to make and create. Making is often confused with tinkering with some basic electronics, but that is just one kind of making. Anything we create and modify is essentially making. In South Africa the maker culture has evolved into something unique. We have passionate people from all walks of life creating, teaching and learning from each other.

South Africa has lots of problems that need solving, and I believe the maker culture is going to play a big part in this. Our maker spaces will become the new schools, and makers our new teachers. It sounds formal and important, but in essence everyone is just having fun (and learning in the process). The maker culture has exploded in the past couple of years, and, where once it was only a few geeks tinkering, it is now considered something for everyone. Our local space has members who are engineers, estate agents, project managers and students. These people come from many different occupations, but they all share the same need to create and learn.

So go ahead! Make something today :)

MICHELLE LISSOOS ThinkAhead education

More and more educators are understanding the importance of hands-on, student-centred, meaningful learning. Instead of viewing learning as the transmission of knowledge from teacher to student, we all agree children learn best when encouraged to discover, design, invent, play and experiment in relation to authentic and real-world scenarios.

Maker education and maker spaces offer a practical solution to fill the gap in schools – the gap of practical, real-life problem solving – ranging from low-tech to hi-tech challenges. Technologies include 3D printing, coding, robotics. The essence of this approach is that students are creators, not just consumers memorising for a test. So students are provided with opportunities that allow them to fail in order to succeed.

The concept also focuses on collaboration and team projects. It is not just a collection of tools, but a collection of ideas, different ages and challenges to be solved. It also introduces students to the idea of entrepreneurship through innovation.

True learning happens when we value curiosity, investigation, experimentation, research and reflection, all of which are key features in making.

ROBYN FARAH Entrepreneur and speaker in teaching and innovation

With regard to being a maker in South Africa, there is huge diversity and dedication among all those involved, from the community organisers to the members. Everyone has huge visions which we are working together to achieve, which is where that sense of collaboration comes in. One person cannot be expected to do it all, nor can one community. Each group is an expert in their own thing, and so collaborating, connecting and sharing is the key to progress and innovation.

MAKING IT A SUPERPOWER

Making encourages non-linear thought and play. This helps you untrain your adult mind, which is conventionally trained to need a plan and to know what the end goal is.

This is a killer creative superpower as it gives you confidence to make it up as you go along without judgement. This is something we've lost in our competitive, goal-oriented world, which ambitious adults need to return to, because we had it, but as you enter the convergent world of immediate response it shrinks and can disappear altogether.

Some things we've learned over the years, but as you can tell from the South African maker community everyone has their own approach and process, which is informed by the people taking part.

- There is no teacher in this space, only a facilitator (if in a school this is the 'teacher'). It's about self- and peer-to-peer learning, so it's important to resist stepping in and wanting to show how it's done or 'help'.

- If the makerthon is about encouraging creativity, it seems best to have broad themes and not specific briefs. Wanting a specific solution or outcome is really a pitch or a business incubator and the two shouldn't be confused. Being prescriptive kills creativity and the playfulness needed to establish confidence is lost.

- In the South African context making is also used as a means to encourage innovation and entrepreneurship. For this to be effective you cannot just create a space and expect an instant start-up community. The support structure needed is complex and needs management who understand the messy process of entrepreneurship and can be fluid and bespoke, according to the need at hand.

- Making is also an amazing community builder, whether it's about bridging cultures, ages, disciplines, introverts and extroverts. When you're working under a little pressure (hackathon/makerthon) overnight there's nothing like fatigue and laughter and comfort eating to bond a group.

South Africa is a unique country with unique challenges and opportunities. Having a thriving maker culture that can bring people together, build confidence, teach critical thinking and even help kick-start entrepreneurship makes making a mega-superpower for us!

SHARED NOISES

By Lucas Abela, Musician

I'm a free-noise musician who makes stuff to make noises with, instrument building being a big part of international noise underground culture. For us, part of the challenge is to create new and different ways to make noise that other players don't use by making or reappropriating stuff. I use the expression free noise to describe my work as I believe what I do to be more in the tradition of free jazz than the noise for noise's sake, wall of sound approach of some of my peers. I prefer my noise experience to be more sculptural, abstract and sometimes, even if just by chance, musical. This is the story of how I came to make noise and the process of discovery that led me to make noise the way I do, and ultimately an attempt to pass on my philosophy on how creativity worked for me. I hope it may be useful to you, whatever your pursuits.

THE ACCIDENTAL NOISE MAKER

I came to noise making quite inadvertently after rolling my Kombi van on Mount Tamborine on the Gold Coast hinterland. It was quite the accident; the van flipped a full 360 to land back on its wheels and I just kept driving. Although still mechanically sound, the body was a write-off, the top having caved in a bit. So I bought another dead VW with a decent body and transplanted the engine and, while I was at it, the radio. Not being an electronics whizz, I must have done something wrong, as instead of picking up radio the car itself became amplified. Somehow, by accident, I had turned my radio into every noise maker's best friend, the contact microphone!

Most people would fix such a thing, but I liked it that when you turned on the windscreen wipers it would send a loud screech through the speakers, and that basically any motion inside would be interpreted by the radio as some kind of distorted noise. The system was quite unpredictable but always fun. My first thought was to share, so I started doing drive-by recitals, pulling up into crowded bus stops to make noise for the waiting passengers and then driving off. That was my introduction to the love of noise making, a weird vocation that I've managed to sustain myself on for the last 25 years or so.

FROM NOTHING SOMETHING GROWS

After my Kombi van sparked my interest, I started looking for other ways to make noises, but being dead broke and living in said van my gear choices were slim. Luckily for me it was the early nineties and for some reason everyone was chucking out their old record players, so there were plenty of decks on the streets for the taking. As a bored teenager, I had modified records for fun, drilling off axis holes and cutting them up and reassembling them, but now I saw an opportunity to modify the turntables themselves, and at minimal expense. My favourite decks were the old-fashioned 'ten to seventy-eight' players you'd find built into furniture, and the first thing I built had three of these platters mounted into one box. I decided almost immediately to do away with tone arms (partly due to the fact that when you spotted a deck on the street it was far easier just to remove the cartridge head than take the entire thing, leaving me with plenty of carts to work with), favouring instead multiple styli on flexible wire arms that could be bent and placed all over the records. One technique I enjoyed was lining them up in rows to build record player centipedes, which produced a vinyl version of a tape delay, all the styli playing a single groove simultaneously.

These bendable wire arms evolved into a stylus glove made by mounting styli onto the end of each finger of a silver ladies' dress glove so I could more literally scratch the records. Having the stylus at your fingertip allowed for a far more nuanced scratch technique. With a gentle back and forth action you could achieve a more warbled variation of the audio; it wasn't just the sound of running the record back and forth – the effect was far more subtle, taking just the slightest wriggle with your fingers while inside the groove. Honestly, I've never heard anything like it before or since, and, since I didn't bother to record any of this (recording never having been a motivating force behind what I do), I'm not sure I will ever hear it again.

SOLVING MISADVENTURE TO YOUR ADVANTAGE

When I played I used to get a little overenthusiastic, especially considering that, back then, I was performing on radio most of the time. This enthusiasm tended to break my styli, so I started sticking sewing machine needles into the cartridges instead. After that I discovered any sharp object would do, and I started playing records with knives and swords. I eventually did away with the turntables altogether, replacing them with high-speed industrial motors that had saw blades and grinding stones attached instead of records to develop a scraping percussive style of turntablism.

As you may have noticed by now, one idea leads to another to the point where what you're doing starts to change into something else. By this point, my use of turntables had become something that barely resembled what most understood turntablism to be. I was no longer using tonearms or decks – all that was left was one small part, the cartridge, which I attached to skewers, knives, springs and all manner of items which I'd still collectively call styli. This evolution of ideas continued leading to styli swordfights and amplified trampolining, among other variations, before I finally discovered my now signature instrument: shards of amplified glass.

Even this was a gradual evolution that started during my first ever overseas tour in Japan in 1997. I couldn't travel with my instruments and had to rebuild my motorised turntables in Osaka. Unfortunately (or perhaps fortunately), the motors I bought weren't as strong as the instrument I'd left behind in Australia, and every time I tried to play the surfaces with the amplified turkey skewers I was using at the time the motors couldn't cope – the friction stopped them from spinning. So out of sheer desperation to make some kind of sound I resorted to sticking these skewers in my mouth and began manipulating them with my lips instead.

It was a revelation – after years of trying to find the most organic way to perform free noise, I discovered that if I vibrated my styli this way I'd achieve the purest, most pristine and accurate way of exporting the music in my head to the real world. So for the next few years I began to concentrate on vocally manipulating various metal objects – until one fateful evening in Sydney in 2003 when, while soundchecking a garden hoe, I noticed some broken glass in the corner of the room. I hooked it up to my mic for a little test, loved it, debuted it that night. I haven't looked back since.

Sonically the glass was far superior. The substance resonated with far more beauty than I could ever muster from the cold-sounding metal I had been using. When you think about it, the glass is the natural conclusion of my turntable work, it to me being nothing more than a giant diamond-tipped stylus vibrated with my mouth instead of a groove.

Although I've exclusively played glass as my preferred instrument for live performance since 2003, the evolution hasn't stopped. Materiality is one thing, but technique is another, and I continue to this day to wrench new sounds from the shards as I experiment with both vocal technique and audio processing to get the best results from this unlikely instrument. My technique is getting so good that maybe it's got to the point where it's no longer a noise instrument, as I can now play everything from bass rhythms to harmonic melodies.

SHARED EXPERIENCES

Since I had found my perfect instrument, the experimenter inside me had to keep exploring new ways to make sound, turning its attention to participatory instruments. As a noise maker I've always felt noise music as an art form is far more rewarding to play than merely observe. Sure, it's fun being surrounded by vibrating air so all-consuming and intense it seemingly nullifies all other aural activity. However, it's another thing entirely to create that physical presence, producing ginormous textures of pure sound by manipulating the very atmosphere around you with nothing more than your lips, a shard of glass and some carefully chosen electronics. It's simply an addictive experience I need to partake in whenever possible, and one I wish upon others.

It's this philosophy that has steered my work with participatory sound sculptures, or, to describe my installations more accurately, large-scale noise instruments devised for musical play that switch roles between audience and performer to give people a taste of the joy that is cause and effect noise making.

This is essentially the fundamental motivation behind the work: to create experiential situations that inadvertently place the audience in a performing role. To do this, I employ situational aesthetics that entice people to engage with the instruments that provide fun, tangible experiences that are layered with purposeful goals requiring focused engagement. For this purpose I've found one method to be highly successful: pinball.

THE FAMILIARITY AMBUSH

I use people's familiarity with the pinball experience to lure them into playing what are in fact noise instruments disguised as pinball machines. By appropriating pinball, I tap into an affinity people have with these much-loved amusements. Once at the controls, audiences seem to possess an innate understanding of the language of the game, the tactile format containing a certain level of intuitiveness that provides audiences with a palpability that sparks immediacy. This tends to be true no matter who encounters the machines; I've witnessed children, the elderly and everyone in between take to the machines with instinctive fervour. Even after distorting the game's iconic form, crafting highly unconventional multiplayer cabinets, game signifiers like flippers, ball shooters, slingshots and pop-bumpers are all that's needed for people to get it, and little instruction is needed.

I initially stumbled onto the concept of using arcade formats as sound installation instruments when I developed my first installation, the Vinyl Rally. Originally conceived as an instrument, where I would drive a remote-control race car with a stylus mounted underneath around a stage covered in old records, this initial idea evolved into a video arcade driving game simulation, like Sega Rally but set in the real world. It allowed the audience to drive the remote-control cars from their point of view across a giant track constructed from old vinyl records while sitting in old video racing cabinets.

This was when I first noticed how the arcade format brought down people's defences when getting involved with interactive art. It bypassed the 'do-this-and-this-happens' passiveness of most work I've experienced in the field and let people loose on the work. Kids especially are drawn to it, which to me was the clincher as they are usually the ones dragging their parents out of the galleries; I knew if I had them onside I was onto something. I thought about making other real-world video games but something troubled me about the screen culture of our time, and then the idea for pinball pianola pretty much appeared in my mind.

IT'S A VISION THING

Imagine a Frankenstein experiment that combined pinball with an upright piano, that has a playfield with twenty flippers all lined up as one big smile wired up to a keyboard so you can volley pinballs back and forth against the piano's exposed strings. Well, that's pretty much the first pinball machine I set out to build, and, mind you, without any previous pinball building experience. I started off by buying a wreck of an old WWF Royal Rumble machine, just to pull apart and get a sense of how it all worked. It was pretty daunting; under the bonnet the modern pinball machine looks pretty complicated. However, by looking closely, I sussed that if you take away the game's computing parts it's basically just electro-mechanical solenoids set off by triggers.

So I stripped down an upright piano to its bare soundboard and constructed a pinball cabinet around it. When I first powered it up I had just finished wiring up the playfield's twenty flippers and proudly turned it on, only to have all my wiring go up in flames, as I didn't really understand the amps involved and was using a wire gauge totally unfit for the task. That's the thing about trial and error self-teaching; Pinball Pianola took me six months to build, while my latest effort and seventh machine, BassBalls, which is technically far more complicated, only took two. With each machine I learn and the process becomes easier, but at the same time with each machine I learn something new and the machines become more complicated.

AUDIO AUGMENTATION

These games are not just instruments/pinball hybrids, as a big part of the fun of noise making is manipulating audio signal with electronic processors. I also like to incorporate audio effects into the machines in order to augment the sounds the instruments create and provide a bit of aural variety for players. This is how a pinball game is turned into a noise instrument. Initially these effects could only be turned on and off using pinball targets, but more recently I've developed (along with my electrical engineer friend Dan Stocks) a set of custom circuits designed as pedal hacks specifically for use in my pinball games. Essentially, they hotwire each control aspect of the pedals either to bypass the effect, switch modes or to change a potentiometer's setting by stepping through four pre-set resistances each time a switch is engaged. When you consider all the different possible combinations that can be dialled in this way a game can have literally millions of different possible effects settings, all randomly selected during game play. When idle the machines are typically quiet or droning, depending on the effects settings at any given time. It's only when the audience engages that the machines come alive aurally, each designed for hands-on, up close and personal experiences.

The cause and effect musical challenges situated within the games employ random compositional techniques steered along by game play. Structurally, the noise produced, while partially random, closely follows audience interactions. This is what I want my audience to appreciate the most as the sonic vibrations produced by the machine physically pass through the cabinet up into their fingertips. The sensation should give the player a sense of steward-ship over the instrument and an ownership of the noises produced, feelings resembling the satisfaction felt when completing a tradi-tional pinball challenge or playing with effects pedals. So, as a player aims and strikes a particular target, and the speakers respond in kind with the reward of noise, they own that moment, giving them a dual perspective as both the sound's audience and creator.

DO TO GET DONE

So, as you can see, my creative process is more like a stream of consciousness discovery, where one idea leads to the next, becom-ing more elaborate with time as knowledge evolves. My noise making started with turntables, a tried and trusted method that had been used many times before, from the Dadaists to John Cage, but from there it became something else all my own. Imagine if I had stopped myself from using turntables just because I knew it had been done before. My personal take on it wouldn't have evolved into glass playing or my work with pinball.

*

This is why I think it's important that before doing anything creative you understand that everything hasn't been done until you yourself have tried it, as everyone brings something different to the table. One person experimenting with an idea will never result in the same thing as another person experimenting with the exact same idea, unless, of course, someone teaches them the experiment. This is essential to my thoughts on what makes a person more creative. To me, self-learning is by far the best way, as it tends to lead to differentiation between ideas, even when the initial thoughts are similar. You see, if people are taught, they tend to replicate . . . which is dull. But if people *discover* . . . well, the results will ultimately vary.

Let me put it this way; if you gave two people a guitar and sent them off individually to learn to play without instruction, they would both return with their own idiosyncratic playing styles. Alternatively, if you taught them to play you would just have another two guitarists. So the best way to do anything is to start doing that thing – and by that I don't mean Google 'how do record players work'; I suggest starting by pulling one apart instead. When I first started hacking decks I probably wouldn't have thought of replacing a stylus with a sewing machine needle if I had been taught how a stylus worked. Sure, my solution was crude, but it was that act that led onto the knives and ultimately the glass. Creation is a learning process that happens in steps, each act of creation leading to the next. I'd prefer you try adding blue paint to yellow to discover green for yourself than be taught the colour wheel. It's a short cut to knowledge, but if you think that way you may as well just buy a finished painting.

HOW MAKING MAKETH THE CREATIVE

By Lizi Hamer, Regional Creative Director at Octagon

The greatest creative geniuses are prolific, an iterating clan that make and experiment – but can the average Joe take a leaf out of their book?

A creative mind does not work 9–5; instead it is whirring, buzzing and connecting dots 24/7. Creative minds invent thoughts and ideas when no one is watching; in fact, they themselves might not even be concentrating. It's incredible to behold.

But rather than just observe, I believe we all need to roll up our sleeves and make for ourselves, because, after all, when we get our hands dirty we learn, discover and improve. The very act of making can help develop your problem-solving skills, and in today's busy world, where problems are becoming ever more complex, a good problem solver will always be in high demand.

This chapter will take you through a creative journey of sheer perspiration in making; how running can help run a community and that the power of bringing more shimmy to a dance party can make the experience matter.

*

Great ideas can come suddenly, sometimes in the middle of a run or during a hot shower, but more often than not when you're in the process of making itself. From the depths of the mind a network of brain cells performs an incredible symphony and an idea comes into consciousness. In recent scientific studies it has been shown that when we 'free' the mind of its inhibitions, we can improve our problem-solving abilities. To free the mind is to stop the logical processing our brains conduct and allow the subconscious to make random associations, unnatural connections, the blind leaps that allow for incredible idea generation. The act of making makes this happen.

> '*The difficulty lies not in grasping the new ideas but rather in escaping from the old ones.*'
>
> – John Maynard Keynes

Our brains hold onto the previously learned solutions and become inhibited by them. As a creative leader I have been exploring a more experimental approach to my creative process: using the freeing and flooding of the mind through the act of making to alter the brain's inhibitions, to build upon ideas and perpetually move forward. Making more again, and learning from it.

Let me tell you the story of one such journey.

ACT ONE: RUNNING

The sky was a deep purple, the wind piercing, there wasn't a soul for miles. I sprinted up the cliff-top hill from Bronte; my thighs screamed and the loud beating of my heart filled my ears. As I rounded the corner, the endorphins were released . . . euphoria flooded through me. Aha! The 'runner's high'. After twenty kilometres of running along the cliff-tops this moment was magic, and I felt as free at that moment as I had at any time in my life. I glided over the next few kilometres with my senses heightened, my attention drawn to the smells of the foliage, the colour of each ocean wave, the sound of the cockatoos squawking. A hard run, finished well.

My triathlon coach had spent the winter teaching me how to race; through understanding the limits of my body, both by how I physically felt and by tracking my data on a Garmin sports watch, I could optimise my performance. (This was 2011, pre-Fitbit and before personal data was as readily accessible as it is nowadays.) I learned how to pace my run in order to maintain an optimal heart rate, allowing me to achieve a negative split – to run faster over the second half of the distance. The data I would capture on each run taught me to understand my body better, and allowed me to measure how well I was progressing.

But over time I started to feel the data was only telling half of my athletic story. I wanted to capture the pain of hill sets, the challenge of early mornings, those stunning sunrises, blisters and sugar shots, as well as the sense of camaraderie with my friends. Because running to me is not just about the race – it's about that feeling of freedom, balance and a sense of purpose.

*

So I began capturing more than just the measurements of pace, distance and heart rate. I observed the people I ran with, the conversations we had, the music that lifted my spirits, as well as my knees – even the sights and smells I experienced. I began to take photographs and short videos of those moments. I experimented with the data and imagery, building visuals of our mornings together.

I shared the images and graphics with the training group, which not only gave me a sense of achievement, but also gave us all a tangible reminder of the morning's effort. My running crew called them 'visual high fives'. And, of course, it wasn't long before I was asked to personalise the artwork for each athlete so they could share their richer world with their friends.

By making I learned:
About how to interpret data to help me run faster, and also how to link data with emotions and experiences to tell stories. I was highly passionate about the subject matter so it felt easy to make work surrounding it. I would recommend that focusing on things you are passionate about is a great place from which to start making.

This project made me notice details of my sport and allowed me to be more present. I observed how people responded to the artwork and the power of personalisation. Let's be honest: not too many people cared about my Garmin reading, but when this same data was transformed into a graphic story, I was able to capture the attention of a far wider audience. I discovered that the blending of data and emotion makes a strong story.

ACT TWO: SHESAYS

Have you ever listened to someone speak while sitting on the edge of your seat, your mind bubbling with inspiration and ideas? Not knowing whether to write every word down, cheer loudly, ask questions or just hope to try and absorb it all?

My enthusiasm for interesting, smart and groundbreaking speakers brought me into the SheSays fold. SheSays is a global creative network for women. They run free events that encourage and support more women into the creative, tech and communication industries. Why? Because we all want to see more women at the top. Creativity thrives on different voices and women are still poorly represented.

But when I first went to SheSays I started at the back of the room, attending sessions, listening to speakers and only occasionally having the courage to ask a question. I realised that events were good but seemed to exist as a moment in time, and the sentiment was short-lived, felt only by those who attended the event.

One evening as a speaker took to the stage I started designing the quotes and statements the speaker shared.

'I am not a small pink version of a man.'

'The most practical tool for generating ideas remains a circle of humans around a table talking shop.'

I found I had an intuitive skill for capturing the speaker's sentiments and expressing their ideas. I was able to process their thoughts and consolidate them into short statements. Each of these statements I then designed into graphic layouts at the speed of the conversation, creating a far bigger impact than a 140-character Tweet ever would. I was able to share the quotes and layouts in real time, engaging audiences both at the venue and online.

I made a lot of these graphics, and, trust me, not all of them worked. But the ones that did were shared further and far more quickly than a simple post would have been – they seemed to develop a life of their own, ending up in news feeds across the world. I often heard from members of the community who couldn't attend, as they explained how they followed the session and learned from the conversation. The pieces were popular with the speakers, too. Using the generosity of design, I was giving back to the speaker in an open forum by showcasing their best sound bites. The reward of having their speech designed built my connection to the speakers and in turn gave them new ways of sharing their message in full colour.

These graphics became a trademark of the SheSays events and I was invited to capture the 'character of the night' – the most interesting speaker each evening. Bringing the event to life in real time allowed us to amplify the reach of the event beyond just the people in the room. My artwork gave women simple and effective statements to show the world what they stood for. Giving the conversation a tangible form allowed women to share their most important moments with others. My making had helped the SheSays network to be stronger and more engaged.

Moving from the back of the room to the front, I now proudly run the SheSays Singapore chapter. We continue to build a community of strong women who are willing to connect with challenging topics and support one another. I have moderated countless panels of exceptional women, bringing to life their stories of impact so we can all learn from them.

By making I learned:

The power of iteration; to make a change you need to make a lot and make often. You need to keep making until you have a range of options and ideas, because until you have a range you don't have a base across which to compare. You can only improve and learn by crafting your skills, which involves hours and hours of making. Making to the point of idea exhaustion opens you to new ways of thinking. Once you have learned about iteration you must then learn how to be a curator. The art of a great creative is to understand what to delete.

Creating artwork for SheSays didn't just expand my network, it pushed me to expand my knowledge of tools and creative resources so that I could make artwork at a more prolific rate and to higher standards. The beauty of live storytelling elevated our SheSays events and helped amplify important messages surrounding female empowerment.

ACT THREE: HEINEKEN SOUND EXPERIMENTS

Your heart is beating a million miles an hour. The club is illuminated, it's hot, it's sweaty. The beat of the music starts to build. You are surrounded by good friends. Your arms are in the air. The beat keeps building. The whole club is moving. The night is incredible . . . The music rises, then boom! The music drops and the entire audience feels it as one.

Remember those nights of heart-pumping anticipation? When you were carefree, when 'your' song came on and you felt you would live forever. How do you capture *that* and share it with someone?

Let me introduce you to the Heineken Sound Experiments, a project my agency team created to push the boundaries of how you could experience music beyond just listening to it. In the Experience Age we worked with Heineken to create a series of interactive events across seventeen Asian cities, bringing together an incredible collaboration of world-class DJs and audiovisual performance artists. Each year we focused on exploring one question. Year One's was, 'can you see music?'

The Year One concept started with unique visuals and projection mapping that was designed in real time to the beat of the music, the space of the club and in response to the movement and exhilaration of the dance floor. It was all brought to life through a giant orb that hung above the dance floor, responding to the movement below.

*

As we developed the project, I knew from my past making that we needed to engage our audience with the emotion of the night. I needed to craft the story for each person attending the event and capture their evening. I began exploring and collating the emotions I'd felt in theatres, the work of emerging artists across Asia, the experience of tech in places such as SXSW and as much research as I could into new interpretations of data.

Through this process the dots started connecting to the experience I had creating the data artworks in athletics, as well as the live storytelling of SheSays. My current creativity built on the previous parts I'd made. More inputs, more connections, more ideas.

So we created the 'Heineken DataSelfie'. Each attendee was gifted an exclusive app which turned their mobile phone into a tracking device, measuring just how much they responded physically and emotionally to the music and visuals. But the DataSelfie needed to go deeper than just their dancing data, it needed to build a more emotional story, so built into the app the capturing of more environmental elements – the music, their friends, the night's peaks and the visual surroundings.

From the lessons of live storytelling I knew we needed the app to provide feedback in real time, showcasing the responsive nature of the event and inspiring the user to become more involved with the experiment. The app provided countdowns to major moments of the night, keeping the user in the right place at the right time – helping them build and share their best story.

*

From the data collected we delivered a personalised circular sound wave: a visual representation of their night. After the experience of creating the athletics artwork, I wanted the precise data to be beautiful, giving a scientific feel but with a symbolic message. In the DataSelfie App, individuals could explore their night by scrolling through their sound wave to reveal a deeper story including the visuals that stimulated them the most, the music of the evening, images of them and their friends and the capture of the Heineken Moment – when we dropped the most exhilarating track and visuals of the night.

The DataSelfie became a personal memento, capturing every attendee's most memorable moments in one place and ensuring they could relive their night. We gave partygoers the tools with which to gloat about the experience, so they could share their dance-floor glory and gain social status, building the reputation of the event.

Heineken Sound Experiments captured the hearts of over 50,000 live music fans in seventeen cities across thirty-six events in 2016. And we created thousands of DataSelfies, allowing 12.5 million people to 'see' the music that mattered to them most.

You can only imagine how amazing it felt to help all these people share the equivalent of their 'runner's high' in all its glory. And it would not have been possible without the knowledge I had gleaned from constant making.

By making I learned:
How to notice the connections between projects, no matter how

big or small. All the things you make equip you with new ways of looking at problems. They will build different skill sets and open you to developing ideas and thinking in more robust ways. You will see the connections that inform the creative process.

Louis Pasteur told us we must have a 'prepared mind'. Being able to have a prepared mind takes effort; you must discover the ability to make mistakes, to try alternatives and to stay optimistic. I learned that I needed to put myself in the best frame of mind to connect new dots and have fun with the experimentation. By making one thing, we influence the next; the more you make, the richer you become.

THE CLOSING ACT

The power of making is threefold.

Firstly, when you create work you make more things for your 'spare parts' pile', an essential part of any creative tool kit. It's often years between the experimentation phase, the creation of something and when you use it, but your spare parts' pile will ensure you always have lots to tinker with and build upon.

Secondly, the physical act of making allows your mind to wander. It's a creative person's hot shower. Making gives the subconscious time to play, to go beyond simply the first thought. It opens the mind to more 'Aha!' moments. Flooding the mind with information allows you to see connections you wouldn't have seen before and equips you with new ways to dream up novel concepts.

Thirdly, making starts you on the creative confidence cycle. The very act of making and the lessons that come from each experience embolden you to take more risks. Plus there is nothing more satisfying than completing a project and the smile you receive when it's shared.

And so my advice about all this is: start making. Make things about the stuff you love and the stuff you hate. Do it yourself and get your hands dirty, so you can see how the pieces fit together. Learn how to shape your ideas in your own way. Your way is unique, and human. Your growth in confidence, space to subconsciously think and the physical building of pieces will set you on your journey to creative brilliance. Be brave. It's the future.

HACKER

INTRODUCTION

By Daniele Fiandaca, Co-founder of
Utopia & Creative Social

When Sir Dave Brailsford was appointed general manager of the new British-based Team Sky in 2010, he faced an extremely tough job. No British rider in history had ever won the Tour de France. Alongside setting a CORE Principle (which stands for Commitment, Ownership, Responsibility and Excellence), he and his team set about improving every single thing that impacts an athlete's performance by 1 per cent. His belief was that if you make these small improvements across the board, then you will make a significant improvement in overall performance.

They started by optimising the things that most teams focused on improving: their weekly training programme, the ergonomics of the bike seat, the weight of the tyres and the nutrition of riders.

Brailsford and his team didn't stop there. They spent a lot of time searching for 1 per cent improvements in tiny areas that had been overlooked by almost everyone else. A great example is their approach to sleeping arrangements during the Tour de France. During the Tour, riders race for twenty-one days, sleeping in a different hotel every night. They don't know ahead of time what kind of beds they'll be sleeping in, and the quality of sleep can vary widely, thus impacting performance. So Brailsford and his team created bespoke bedding (a bed, a mattress and a pillow) for each athlete; the team then went ahead of the riders and replaced the bedding in their rooms so that every night each rider slept in a bed designed specifically for them.

They did this for every single aspect of performance – they even tested for the most effective type of massage gel and hired a surgeon to teach the athletes about proper hand-washing so as to avoid illnesses during competition (and his Team GB team decided not to shake hands during the Olympics). And they saw opportunities for improvement everywhere – not just in relation to the athletes themselves. They redesigned the meeting process, for instance, so that every meeting was far more efficient (and they consequently had more time to spend with the athletes), and they painted the floor of the bike maintenance area to better spot any impurities/dust that could impact the aerodynamics of the bike.

Brailsford set himself a target of winning the Tour de France within five years. Bradley Wiggins became the first British winner of the Tour de France in 2012. In that same year Brailsford coached the British Olympic cycling team to eight gold medals, making it one of the most successful teams in history, winning 70 per cent of the track cycling gold medals available.

Sir Dave Brailsford is a hacker. Not a computer hacker, a term synonymous with the word hacker in popular culture thanks to things like the 1995 film of the same name, the activist group Anonymous and recent TV series *Mr Robot*, but, rather, someone who enjoys the intellectual challenge of creatively overcoming and circumventing limitations of systems to achieve novel and clever outcomes.

History is littered with example of hackers. In fact, the earliest known incidence of hacking can be found around 330 BC. For those who don't know their history, Alexander the Great became king of the ancient Greek kingdom of Macedon and by the age of thirty had created one of the largest empires of the ancient world.* However, he had a problem. He was as vain as you would expect a leader of an empire to be, and hated the fact that not everyone knew what he looked like. There were not enough sculptors in the kingdom to make enough statues of him. So it is said he put his face on every coin.†

Florence Nightingale was also a hacker. While she was a nurse treating injured soldiers in Turkey during the Crimean War, she discovered that most of the soldiers who died did so not from their initial wounds but from infection or diseases they acquired in the hospital. As a result she made sure that everyone working there washed their hands frequently and kept everything clean; this led to a dramatic decrease in fatalities. It is amazing to think it took more than 150 years for hospitals to extend the practice to hospital visitors as well.

---

* According to Wikipedia the Macedonian Empire covered 3.5 per cent of the world, which would make it the twenty-second largest empire in history.

† Some historians believe it was in fact Hercules on the coin, but why let the truth get in the way of a good story?

*

Julia Child was a hacker. During the Second World War, she baked cakes that acted as a shark repellent to stop sharks exploding weapons targeting German U-boats.

Graffiti artists in seventies New York were hackers – they worked out that the best way to make sure the whole city could see their art was by tagging subway cars.

Mayor Rudy Giuliani was also a hacker. When he looked to combat crime in New York after he became mayor, he implemented the 'Broken Windows theory', which had been tested in small neighbourhoods in New York City, across the entire city. The Broken Windows theory was that, rather than ignoring petty crime and focusing on more serious forms of crime, you actually did everything you could to stamp out the petty crime, which included cleaning up the neighbourhood by painting over graffiti and fixing the broken windows. His hypothesis was that by creating neighbourhoods that people could be proud of, crime would fall. And it did.

Ann Makosinski is a hacker working right now to find innovative solutions to her problems. She couldn't study at night because there was no electricity in her house, so she invented a light bulb using a hollow aluminium tube which is powered by body heat.

To a certain extent the best way to understand what we mean by hacker is to go back to the original definition of 'to hack' – to cut with rough or heavy blows. Hacking is about taking a problem and cutting it with repeated blows in order to make it better. In our previous book* Gareth Kay, Co-founder at ChapterSF, referred to this aspect of hacking: 'Hacks, by definition, are more effective. They take big complicated problems that can be more easily solved, whatever the solution takes. As a result, they remove the gap between the commercial imperative and the creative solution.'

Perhaps my favourite definition of hacker was given to me by John Wilshere, Founder of Smithery: 'A hacker is someone who always assumes that one part is broken.' By assuming that one part is broken, you have to find what is broken and then you can focus on fixing it, thus making it better.

Hacking is a continuous process, and ultimately reflects a state of mind. Indeed, one of the original definitions of hacking, coined by MIT's Tech Model Railroad Club in 1959, was 'an article or project without constructive end'.

And while the definition of hacking provided in this book is relatively new, it has actually been pervading popular and business culture for quite a while now.

The term 'life hack' was first invented in 2004 at a technology conference by Danny O'Brien to describe the embarrassing short cuts IT professionals made to get the work done, and this defini-tion has now evolved to encompass any trick, short cut, skill or novelty method that increases productivity and efficiency. Now-adays, it's possible to spend a lot of time finding and testing

---

* *Hacker, Maker, Teacher, Thief: Advertising's Next Generation* edited by Ana Andjelic, Daniele Fiandaca and Gareth Kay

productivity hacks to become more efficient with your time. For example, Tony Hsieh, founder of Zappos, uses yesterday's emails as today's to-do list. Dave Bedwood, creative partner at CHI&Partners, splits his day into two, with the morning focused solely on input (emails, reading, being inspired, etc.) and the afternoon focused solely on output (delivering work).

There is no doubt that technology has been at the root of much of the growth in this hacking subculture. For example, growth hacking has been a significant factor in the creation of some of the world's biggest unicorns (start-ups worth over $1 billion). Growth hacking, as defined by Wikipedia, is a marketing technique developed by technology start-ups, which uses creativity, analytical thinking and social metrics to sell products and gain exposure.

One of the most famous examples of a growth hack can be found back in 1996, at a start-up called Hotmail – one of the first web-based email services. Pre-launch one of the investors suggested putting 'PS I love you. Get your free email at Hotmail' at the bottom of each email. The suggestion was initially given short shrift by the founders. However, after an underwhelming first week post-launch, they relented and included a shortened clickable version on every email. Within five weeks they had two million users, and the rest is history (two years later they were sold to Microsoft for $400 million). It's highly likely that you yourself have been helping to spread the word about another product in a similar way ever since it was launched in 2007. The difference is that by including 'Sent from my iPhone' on your emails, you were building the iPhone brand. That's a lot of free ads over the last decade.

Other famous growth hacks include the code that allowed YouTube videos to be embedded in other web pages, Airbnb making it easy for users to list their property on Craigslist (by building a bot that visited Craigslist, snagged a unique URL, input the listing info, and forwarded the URL to the user for publishing) and Dropbox giving you extra online file storage if you recruit a friend.

While growth hacking is often associated with technology, I prefer to look at it from a human perspective: how can you make people's customer experience better? (Uber's integration into Google Maps is a brilliant example of that.) How can you get your users to become part of your marketing team? (The best Kickstarter campaigns do this brilliantly by offering you extra rewards if they hit stretch goals – this encourages the backers to share the campaign with as many people as they can.)

Culture hacking, on the other hand, refers to the making of small changes to create cultural change in companies. Annicken R. Day covers culture hacking in detail in her chapter 'Using Hacking to Build Better Business'. I will never forget what my wife, who is people and culture director at a big advertising agency, said the first time I introduced her to the concept of culture hacking: 'So that's been what I have been doing my whole career.' My wife, like me, is a hacker.

*

It is certainly worth stating that the concept of hacking has existed in other cultures all over the world for years. When I first introduced the concept of hacking to a room of Indians in Mumbai, they all looked at me with blank faces. When I asked what was wrong, they said, 'But that's what we do every day. We just call it Jugaad'. In Brazil they have a word, 'Jeitinho', which means 'finding a way to accomplish something by circumventing or bending the rules or social conventions'. A fantastic example of this is the racing driver Nelson Piquet, who used to heat up his tyres before a race using a hairdryer before warming up the tyres became standard practice.

So how do you become a hacker? Well, first and foremost, hacking is a state of mind, and while you may not have considered yourself a hacker before you picked up this book, you might just find that you already have many of the characteristics of one. Are you always looking for ways to make things better? Are you open to new ideas? Do you have a natural curiosity to learn and teach? Do you believe that if you don't fail it probably means you aren't pushing yourself hard enough? Are you always looking for new people who can help solve your problem? If some of these resonate, you are already halfway to becoming a hacker.

And while hacking is an innate skill set for many, it can also be learned by getting into the habit of challenging yourself to make and test changes in everything you do. Rather than just doing what you did last time, ask yourself how you might make something better. Look at your job and ask yourself: 'What would making everything better by two per cent look like?' Then prioritise, implement and test.

The following chapters will give you a better understanding of this mindset and how you can apply it to problem solving. Annicken explains how culture hacking has helped shape her career and how it can lead you to becoming a better leader. Hugh Garry will explain how your brain hacks the way you think and how you can hack it yourself to allow you to be a better creative thinker. And Ravi Deshpande will tell us more about how Jugaad, a Hindi word which means finding a low-cost solution to any problem in an intelligent way, has helped build one of the most innovative cultures in the world.

Enjoy.

USING HACKING TO BUILD BETTER BUSINESS

By Annicken R. Day, Founder of Corporate Spring

'There is a crack in everything. That is how the light gets in.'
— Leonard Cohen

THE CULTURE HACKER

It was a Friday afternoon, late August 2009. The evenings were still long and light as they are in Norway during the summer months, my favourite season of the year. I was wrapping up for the weekend. It had been a hectic week and I had just finished our three-day New Hire Workshop, the fifth that year. Tandberg, the Norwegian company I worked for, was growing like crazy and we were adding new people in every corner of the world every week. Six to seven times a year we invited all new employees for a three-day 'new hire experience' at the Oslo HQ, where they came to learn about the company, the history, the products, the vision – and, most importantly, about our culture. During the workshop, we made a point of having people work in diverse teams, their titles and roles irrelevant. The Japanese secretary worked on projects with the vice president of sales in the US, the Norwegian engineer solved complex issues together with the South American key account manager. In the evenings everyone socialised and had fun together; the most unlikely friendships and bonds were made, some of them never to be broken.

Some new hires called the experience mind-blowing. Others called it transformational. We just called it 'our way of doing things'. By creating the opportunity for people to *experience* what our company was all about, rather than us just telling them, we demonstrated our values and culture and made it easy for everyone to understand why we did things the way we did, as well as what was expected from each and every one of us.

When we waved the bus goodbye that Friday afternoon, my team and I were exhausted, happy and proud, knowing that once again we had achieved the goal we always set for ourselves: that the new hires' eyes would shine brighter when they left than when they had arrived. It always happened. And it gave me goose bumps every time.

As I returned to the office to get my things, one of the engineers enthusiastically said to me, 'Hey, I've just realised what it is you do'. We had known each other for five years, so I laughed and asked, 'What took you so long?' But I knew there was more to his comment, and was curious to see what would come next.

'You're totally a culture hacker!' he said with a big grin. Coming from an engineer, I knew that was a huge compliment, but I had to admit I had no idea what he was talking about. 'Check out the

Netflix Culture deck. You are not alone,' he said cryptically, wished me a happy weekend and left.

Seven years earlier I had been hired as Tandberg's chief cultural officer, with the job description and mandate to 'take care of the corporate soul'. The role had been initiated by the founder and chairman, who explained in my interview with him: 'We might be a small fish in a big pond now, but we will become a global leader in the video conferencing industry one day. There is only one thing that can stop that from happening and that is if we lose our soul on the way. Your job will be to take care of it.' I fell in love with the company that day.

'The Hacker Way is an approach to building that involves continuous improvement and iteration. Hackers believe that something can always be better, and that nothing is ever complete'.   – Mark Zuckerberg

The night after the New Hire Workshop, with a glass of wine in my hand I opened up my PC, Googled 'Netflix Culture' and found the document my engineer colleague had referred to. It was a 125-slide PowerPoint presentation, originally developed to give Netflix employees a foundational understanding of what it means to work for the company and the kind of attitudes and behaviours that were expected from them. The document has since been read by over seventeen million people and has been called 'the most important document ever to come out of Silicon Valley' by Facebook's COO Sheryl Sandberg.

*

The main message of the deck is that Netflix wanted to foster a culture of freedom and responsibility, that they treated their employees as adults – and expected them to act accordingly. 'With the right people, instead of a culture of process adherence, we have a culture of creativity and self-discipline, freedom and responsibility.' Their strategy was to grow without adding more rules but more high-performing people, who would make the right decisions for the company, without necessarily being told what to do.

Both the Tandberg and Netflix approach to culture was based on common sense; give people responsibility and they will take it, treat them like adults, and they will act like it. However, having worked with multiple organisations around the world over the last ten years, I have learned that common sense isn't very common in the business world.

I hope and believe that is about to change.

WHAT CULTURE IS

Many mistake 'culture' for cookies in a jar, fussball tables, wild parties and other nice perks. Some leaders say that their culture matters, but won't give it proper attention 'until business gets better'. To me that makes as much sense as constructing the foundations of a house after it is built and giving a flower water only if it blossoms.

Corporate culture is how people do things in a company or organisation, their collective mindsets and behaviours, formed by their values and beliefs, whether they are conscious of them or not. Culture is not a stand-alone thing but should be ingrained into every aspect of a company's business. Culture influences how things are done, how decisions are made and how customers are treated. It determines the quality of its services and its products, its reputation and the company's brand.

> *'Always treat your employees the way you want them to treat your best customers.'* — Stephen Covey

Every leader has a simple choice: to be conscious about the culture they need to have in order to achieve their business objectives, or to ignore it and just let the culture develop by chance. Surprisingly, many end up doing the latter.

As management guru Peter Drucker said in the 1960s, 'Culture eats strategy for breakfast.'

Companies with strong, healthy and inspired cultures collaborate better, innovate more and deliver up to 50 per cent better results, they are able to move fast and adapt to constantly changing circumstances.

'Strategies are nothing but a guessing game for a future reality that is impossible to predict', my former Tandberg leader told me. 'With the right kind of culture we can handle anything, come what may.' He was right.

THE NEW WORLD OF WORK

The world is going through some of the biggest transformations we've ever seen.

With digitalisation, automation, globalisation and a new 'digital native' generation soon to take over the workplace, there is a new world of work. Complex problem solving, critical thinking and creativity are, according to the World Economic Forum, some of the most important skills of the future.

According to the 2016 Deloitte Human Capital Trend report, leaders and companies will need to focus on three things in order to survive in the digital age: organisational design, leadership and corporate culture.

In the research, based on 7,000 businesses from 130 countries, Deloitte found that 92 per cent of the companies surveyed said that today's digital world of work has *shaken the foundation* of their organisational structure. Deloitte believes we will see shifts from traditional functional hierarchies to 'networks of teams'. This will require radical changes in how companies are organised and led – not only structurally but also with shifts in mindsets and behaviours, initiated and driven from the top.

Ninety per cent of the companies in the Deloitte study cite leadership as a major problem. While only ten years ago leaders might have got away with 'position/title-based leadership', they will instead now be required to inspire and engage their teams through expertise, passion, energy and empowerment. Many leaders will need to relearn what leadership is, as emotional intelligence, empathy and kindness become as important to the job as IQ and formal competence have traditionally been.

Crucially, 86 per cent of the companies also said that culture is very important, and 82 per cent considered it a competitive advantage. The majority of the 'digital natives', the generation that will soon make up 50 per cent of the working population, say they value great culture, inspiring purpose and meaningful work over formal roles, position and salary. And in spite of traditional beliefs, research shows that this is not only a *generational* thing; this is in fact a *human* thing. According to Gallup, meaningful work and inspiring cultures lead to increased engagement, collaboration, innovation and higher performance for *everyone* in the workplace.

HACKING CULTURE

In 2010 Tandberg was acquired by the American IT giant Cisco. To say there was a culture clash between the entrepreneurial culture of Tandberg and the hierarchical structure of Cisco is an understatement. Cisco had once upon a time been more like Tandberg itself, but it had grown very big very fast without any clear guidelines on what kind of culture they wanted to foster. Thus, systems, structure and control had to a large degree replaced individual initiative and the sense of personal responsibility that once upon a time also had been 'the Cisco Way'. Many employees and leaders felt frustrated and disempowered and thought there was 'nothing to be done to change things'.

*

I decided to prove them wrong.

Over a period of two years, I helped hack multiple team cultures by facilitating the shaping of more self-empowered, autonomous teams. When teams were given ownership for building their own 'tribal' team culture in support of their goals and the overall vision and purpose of the company, they went from a victim attitude to a creator attitude. When mindsets shifted from 'I am one out of 60,000 employees and really can't influence a thing' to 'I am a member of this passionate "tribe", this is how we do things, this is how we can change things and this is why we jump out of bed in the morning', lots of energy, creativity and pride was unleashed. One of the teams experienced a 13 per cent increase in employee engagement, significant cost savings and improved performance over a period of only six months.

To engage and involve entire teams in creating their own 'culture codes' to guide leadership and employee mindsets and behaviours is a very effective way of creating strong and aligned team cultures. After my Cisco years I have helped many other teams and companies around the world to do the same and have over and over again seen the amazing effects of this rather simple approach.

Cultures can indeed be shaped bottom up, but the shaping of them is even more effective when combined with some guidance from the top. Here are six of my favourite 'culture hacks', created by some of the world's most innovative and forward-thinking leaders:

HACKING EMPLOYEE WELLBEING

Why focus on the hours clocked instead of getting the job done, Richard Branson, founder of the Virgin empire, asked himself. As the world is changing and technology allows people to work from anywhere at any time, why keep old-fashioned metrics like 'time spent in the office'? Salaried Virgin employees were told to take whatever time off they felt was appropriate, as long as they were sensible and didn't harm the business.

Richard Branson said he had been inspired by the Netflix Culture deck, too, and when other companies like LinkedIn, Grubhub and even General Electric started following their examples, the case for such a vacation policy was getting increasingly clear: it improved talent acquisition, retention and productivity. While the majority of the employees did not take more vacation than they used to, the feeling that they *could* helped develop a new sense of empowerment, responsibility and overall employee wellbeing.

HACKING COST EFFICIENCY

In Tandberg we had a simple Norwegian sentence that all employees were taught to pronounce: 'Pass på penga' – 'Watch the money'. We did not implement cost control, simply because we believed that people would be more conscious of their spending when they felt trusted rather than controlled. The consequence was that people put their pride in being cost-effective and even made internal competitions like 'who can get the cheapest ticket to New York?' or 'how cheaply can you sleep in Paris?'. The heroes were the ones who found creative solutions to save money, like one of the engineers who signed up for a university course to get student discounts on airline tickets, or the sales guy who always took the night train to customer meetings to save the cost of a hotel room.

Netflix has a similar philosophy called 'Act in Netflix's best interest': trusting employees to spend company money as if it is their own, saving money and time on things like third-party travel agencies and unnecessary cost control.

HACKING PROFITABILITY

'Budgets are not fixed,' Reed Hastings wrote in the Netflix Culture deck. The Netflix approach to budgets is quite different from most companies, who seem to think that 'the budget' is the God-given answer to all their questions.

How many great ideas and initiatives have been stopped because of the six highly discouraging words: 'It is not in the budget'? What if budgets are hindering progress and the whole idea of budgets in fact is becoming redundant?

'Budgeting is fundamentally flawed. The solution is not "better budgeting", but abandoning it and building an alternative management model,' Bjarte Bogsnes writes in his book *Beyond Budgeting*.

The Swedish bank Handelsbanken embraced the principles of *Beyond Budgeting* over forty years ago; with no advance budgets they only judge their branches on two key metrics: customer satisfaction and cost to income ratio. Handelsbanken is one of the most successful and profitable banks in Europe.

HACKING CUSTOMER SERVICE

The online retail business may not be best known for excellent customer service, and that is exactly why Tony Hsieh, founder and CEO of Zappos, an online shoe retailer, decided to create a different kind of online shopping experience. Internally, Zappos call themselves 'a service company that just happens to sell shoes'. In his book *Delivering Happiness*, Hsieh writes that in order to achieve their goal of creating excellent customer service to their customers, Zappos' priority number one was culture:

> *'Our whole belief is that if you get the culture right, most of the other stuff like delivering great customer service or building long-term enduring brand will just happen naturally on its own.'*
> – Tony Hsieh

By hiring the right people, training them well and fostering an environment of happiness in the workplace, Zappos found their way of making customers happier, employees happier and, ultimately, investors happier.

HACKING PRODUCTIVITY

Thierry Breton, CEO of Atos Origin, a Bezons, France-based IT firm with 70,000 employees worldwide, noticed that his employees seemed constantly distracted by the stream of emails they received each day and decided to hack the crack he believed was negatively influencing the company's productivity.

In February 2011, Breton announced that he was banning email, saying he wanted Atos to be a 'zero-email' company within three years. Breton himself had stopped using internal email nearly five years earlier because he found it made him less productive. Instead of using emails, the company built a social network with 7,500 open communities representing the various projects that required collaboration, where employees could choose to enter the discussion on their terms and their schedule.

Three years later Atos hadn't hit 0 per cent email, but the company had reduced overall email by 60 per cent and showed a higher level of productivity and a 50 per cent increase in earnings per share.

HACKING INNOVATION CULTURE

It is becoming increasingly clear to business leaders around the world that 'business as usual' isn't an option anymore, and that the ways in which companies organise, leaders lead and people work are in the midst of a huge transformation.

Professor Vladka Hlupic of Westminster University writes in her book *The Management Shift* that companies that encourage conformity, order and control show lower levels of productivity and innovation than those that build cultures of collaboration, enthusiasm and limitless possibilities.

*

Wharton Professor Adam Grant writes in his book *Originals* that most people are capable of novel thinking and problem solving, if only their organisation would stop pounding them into conformity. The way to hack a culture of innovation is, according to Adam Grant, to build a culture of non-conformity, where the original thinkers and 'corporate rebels' are encouraged to challenge the status quo, and, by doing so, inspiring others to do the same.

THE HACKER'S WAY

To create effective cultures that are able to embrace the ambiguity, uncertainty and complexity of our times, it clearly has its advantages when culture is a priority in every level of the organisation. But even without a direct mandate from the top, people with passion, persistence and courage, who dare to challenge the system and come up with new and innovative solutions to new and old problems, can make – and are making – huge differences in companies around the world. As a participant in one of my culture workshops said: 'If we wait until the execs get the seriousness of the situation to make the necessary changes, there wouldn't be a culture – or a company – to improve anymore.'

When Adam Grant was asked to help unleash innovation and change in that ultimate bastion of bureaucracy, the US Navy, he was amazed to discover how a group of original thinkers were transforming the way the organisation worked. With a bottom-up approach they were creating a culture of creativity and innovation by embracing original ideas and thinkers within their own organisation. A young flyer named Ben Kohlmann had challenged the traditional ways of the US Navy and he and some other 'originals' (also recognised as 'troublemakers') had helped redefine how things should be done. Along the way, Kohlmann had discovered the power of culture. 'Culture is king,' he told Adam Grant. 'When people discovered their voice they became unstoppable.'

What this young flyer had discovered was the ultimate 'culture hacker's way'. Culture hacking is not only about making changes to how things are done; most of all it's about unleashing the greatness already there.

HAVE YOU HAD YOUR BRAIN HACKED RECENTLY?

By Hugh Garry, Director at Storythings

'We'd like everyone in the audience to take out their mobile phones and turn them on. Because we're gonna pick one person from the audience and invite them on stage to video this trick from an angle that will show them how it's done.'

That's how one of my favourite Penn and Teller tricks starts. A blow-by-blow description will not give it credit, so type 'Penn & Teller Cellfish' into Google and spend the next 6:29 minutes watching this beautifully crafted trick. I could now give you a highly detailed account of how it's done, but I won't. Rather, I am going to use it to talk a little about a few pillars of magic that will not only help you piece together how the trick is done but also help you develop your own creative processes.

Great magic can take years to craft. When done well, the performance of a conjuring trick is no less beautiful than a piece of art, music or poetry. Phrases we associate with magic such as 'sleight of hand' suggest a simplicity that belies the effort that goes into a trick's creation. Like artists or musicians, magicians are working with a set of tools appropriate to their field which they rely upon to craft their creations. You're forgiven if rabbits in hats and boxes for sawing people in two instantly spring to mind here as physical props do play their part in a magician's show. But the most valuable tools available to magicians exist in the minds of the audience. Without access to them brilliant magic simply wouldn't happen.

Magicians are the original hackers. They look for flaws in the operating systems of the human brain and exploit them through sleight of hand, misdirection and great storytelling. The combination of skills and flaws produces results so remarkable that even the sharpest among us often find ourselves questioning the reality of what we have just experienced. I use the word 'experienced' rather than 'seen' because the gap between the data that goes in through the eyes and how the brain turns that data into a visual story is where the magic 'experience' truly happens.

Over the last few decades advances in technology have given neuroscientists a window into the workings of the human brain. But long before the technology existed neuroscientists were turning to magicians for insights into the quirks of our behaviour. All the props in the world couldn't produce the spectacle mentioned above if it wasn't for Penn and Teller's deep understanding of how our brains work and how the brain's weaknesses and quirks can be exploited. That performance is a rigid set of pre-planned moments, constructed around these weaknesses, that when strung together by a brilliant narrative creates an illusion, making the impossible appear possible.

*

When it comes to generating ideas we are taught little, if anything, about the role our brain plays in generating them. In fact, throughout my schooling I was never taught where ideas come from. When I got my first Saturday job as a bread delivery boy my boss asked me to come up with some ideas for selling more sandwiches. 'How do you come up with ideas?' I wondered. We didn't have 'How to come up with ideas' lessons squeezed between Geography and Physical Education at our school. When I got a 'proper job' many years later I realised that everything I did was based around coming up with new ideas. But we didn't have workplace training for coming up with ideas. We just had rules for running a brainstorm. So I did my research, and it turns out that although Post-it notes are useful tools, creating the best environment for ideas requires a better understanding of how the brain manages information. As with a magician, props alone won't do the trick.

The magician manages inbound information in two ways. The first is all about attention. Magicians understand how our brain decides what to give attention to. Magicians must control the attention of the audience and in doing so must understand how the brain makes conscious and unconscious decisions about attention. The second is about making connections and how the brain uses heuristics or rules of thumb to make assumptions and predictions based on a small incoming data set. A combination of these facets creates firm ground upon which a magician can begin to craft his trick.

For a trick to work the only ending is the one the magician has been planning for months, or, in some cases years, in advance. The role of the magician is to capture your attention and guide it toward a single outcome. Everything is on rails heading towards a clear destination. From the moment the magician steps onto the stage they take your attention by the hand and walk it along a chosen path. They construct a story to navigate the journey, ensuring your attention is exactly where they want it to be at all times. Like the choice of architecture that shapes what you buy in a supermarket or guarantees the house always wins in casinos, the magician's performance is designed along a set of structural pointers that shout 'HEY – THIS IS WHERE WE WANT YOUR ATTENTION RIGHT NOW'. Every action is a story-driven distraction perfectly plotted to keep your attention away from the mechanics of the trick. Everything outside your frame of vision is a no-go zone. All other routes have to be removed using brilliantly placed curiosity roadblocks. The mind must not wander.

For creativity to flourish the human brain needs the freedom to roam. It has to wander wildly, liberated from rules, routes and reason. It must forget about destinations and simply allow serendipity to steer its course, make connections and discover new solutions. For this to happen we need to shift our state of thinking from conscious to unconscious. We need to go from focused attention to an unfocused state of mind.

Following a well-trodden route with strategically placed attention points along the way will only lead to unsurprising destinations — the exact place the magician wants you to end up. In the context of the workplace, think about the loud colleague in the workshop with his own agenda who continually steers the conversation his way. He manages everyone's attention though volume and personality. Then groupthink kicks in and you end up with the solution he's had up his sleeve the whole time.

Shifting your mental state from 'on-rails thinking' to 'off-rails thinking' requires a new level of awareness of your attentional state. Great ideas happen through shifts of focus – or, rather, changing channel from conscious to unconscious thinking. As counter-productive as it might sound, switching off is the way to turn on the idea generation process in the brain. History is littered with moments of inspiration coming when people are taking time off from thinking about the problem they were trying to solve. When Archimedes shouted 'Eureka' he was taking a bath. Newton saw the apple drop when he was sitting under an apple tree in the garden. Keith Richards came up with the guitar riff for 'Satisfaction' just as he was waking up, while Paul McCartney went one better, coming up with the melody for 'Yesterday' in a dream.

It's a classic Pareto principle problem, namely 20 per cent of the invested input is responsible for 80 per cent of the results obtained. We spend so much time consciously trying to manifest ideas in brainstorms and workshops, yet the best results come when we are doing 'other' things.

There's a simple reason for this. It's all to do with a part of the brain that we put a lot of trust in when perhaps we shouldn't. The brain's prefrontal cortex acts as a selective gating or filtering mechanism that controls information processing. It keeps irrelevant thoughts, perceptions and memories from interfering with a task at hand. It's all about keeping focus, ensuring that only relevant information passes through at a specific time. It does this in order to manage the limited processing power of the brain. You don't want the complete works of Shakespeare running through your head as you're trying to divvy up a restaurant bill. Think of it as the brain's receptionist, primed for efficiency. So, certainly useful at times.

But for creativity to flourish the brain needs randomness. The best ideas are simply a juxtaposition of disparate ones combined in fascinating new ways. This challenges the working methods of the brain's receptionist, which might not think a calligrapher or kitchen appliance sales assistant should be invited to a meeting about computer hardware. Their quest for efficiency and dislike of randomness instantly dismisses them as irrelevant, failing to recognise the role calligraphy and kitchen appliances played in the story of Steve Jobs and Apple. Having dropped out of college, Jobs returned some years later to take a part-time calligraphy course. If it wasn't for that course the Mac would not have had multiple typefaces or proportionally spaced fonts. In fact, Jobs may never have seen the beauty in type at all. Similarly, Jobs spent time studying kitchen appliances on visits to Macy's in Palo Alto, especially the Cuisinart, whose design he loved. Its lines and curves would go on to influence the designs of Apple products for years to come – as would Zen Buddhism, the Polaroid, Bauhaus and the architecture of Joseph Eichler.

So, to get randomness into the meeting, you're going to have to act like a magician and distract the receptionist.

*

Hacking your brain for better ideas is easier than it sounds. It's about finding the distraction sweet spot. You do it all the time without noticing. There is no one hack fits all to finding that sweet spot – you just need to pay attention to what it is you're doing when those unconscious random thoughts rise to the surface. When that happens take note of what you are doing. What sounds can you hear? Where are you? Are you standing still or moving? When you shower, or walk, or swim or run, or whatever it is that flips your brain into the right state for coming up with ideas, you are simply creating that necessary distraction. The white noise of the water or the monotonous rhythm of our steps is enough to occupy the prefrontal cortex while our mind's 'non-thinking' state of consciousness is having an ideas party at the back.

With the quietening of the conscious mind, the volume of our unconscious thought rises. Ideas appear to spring from nowhere, made up from combinations of information you've let into your mind over the course of your entire life. Every book you've read, every film you've watched, every piece of music you've listened to and every piece of art you've enjoyed are all dots waiting to be connected. Like Steve Jobs and his passion for kitchen appliances, Zen Buddhism and Bauhaus, the more diverse the dots you've collected the better ideas the connections make.

Creating magic needs years of practice, as does the process of retraining the brain to open itself up to what it was like to be a child. You need to hack the brain itself and give it a chance to bring to the surface those ideas that are hidden in your unconscious. It is what David Pearl is doing with Street Wisdom (detailed later in the book). For me, swimming is brilliant for switching channel to off-rails thinking. But it's not always convenient, so along with going for walks here are three techniques that have worked for me and I hope will make you better at coming up with ideas and solving problems:

Three ways to hack your mind to create better ideas:

1. DO SOMETHING BORING

By doing something unsatisfying your brain seeks to be engaged. In a recent study by researchers, University of Central Lancashire participants were asked to come up with creative uses for two cups. One group was asked to copy numbers from a phone book while the other just got on with coming up with ideas. By the end of the experiment the ones who had to copy numbers from the phone book were able to come up with more creative uses for the plastic cups.

2. MAKE A MESS

Albert Einstein once said, 'If a cluttered desk is a sign of a cluttered mind, then what are we to think of an empty desk?' While I don't advocate covering your desk with rubbish I would encourage having lots of 'visual stimulation' scattered around for your eyes to fall upon unconsciously. Both the *New York Times* and researchers at Northwestern University ran experiments which found that subjects in a messy room drew more creative pictures or came up with more creative solutions to tasks than subjects in a tidy room. And if that's not enough proof, type 'Steve Jobs Desk' and 'Mark Zuckerberg Desk' into Google Images.

3. BRING THE (AMBIENT) NOISE

Lots of people like to work in silence, while others prefer to don their headphone and crank up the volume. However, research by Ravi Mehta, Rui Zhu and Amar Cheema for the *Journal of Consumer Research*[*] showed that a moderate level of ambient noise induces abstract cognition and consequently enhances creativity. A high level of noise, however, impairs creativity by reducing the extent of information processing.

After years of studying creativity it's easy to understand why so few people are taught how to come up with ideas at school or in the workplace. Coming up with ideas is a messy old affair, one that depends on randomness, daydreaming and a belief that the ideas will appear from nowhere. You have to have faith in a part of the brain you don't control. And, most importantly, you have to believe in magic.

---

[*] Is Noise Always Bad? Exploring the Effects of Ambient Noise on Creative Cognition.

HOW HACKING HELPED BUILD ONE OF THE WORLD'S LARGEST ECONOMIES

*By Ravi Deshpande, Founder and Chairman
at WHYNESS Worldwide*

Anyone who has been to the ancient Indian city of Varanasi must believe in the existence of God. The city is the epitome of disorder, yet, somehow, everything works.

Varanasi represents the spiritual side of India, one that makes peace with the idea that life itself is an illusion. The unstructured way of somehow making things work could either be the handiwork of God or people's instinct to innovate in funny little ways depending on the availability or, rather, unavailability of resources. In this case, the latter is probably true.

People in developing countries with fewer resources, such as in India, have developed the ability to create more from less. They are inclined towards developing sustainable solutions from the limited resources available to them, although they may not always succeed in doing so.

For example, a remote village may not have a constant supply of electricity; however, the families that live there may have access to a low-cost fridge that does not run on electricity – Mitti Cool is a refrigerator made of clay that keeps vegetables fresh for up to five days. Or, for instance, a street might be in need of cleaning, and the solution could be a bicycle that also works as a broom that sweeps the street as you ride the bicycle.

This kind of innovation, which springs from a lack of resources, is called Jugaad in colloquial Hindi and in the Punjabi language. In other words, it is hacking life, the Indian way.

Here it is important to emphasise that the concept of Jugaad, or frugal innovation, which refers to the process of reducing the complexity and cost of an item of goods and its production, is not exclusively Indian. Examples of such thinking can be found in the wealthier West, too.

A small British firm, specialising in 360-degree projections for entertainment, for instance, wanted to reproduce the effect of an airline simulator projected inside a dome, for festival-goers to relax inside. But the simulator was so expensive that it was out of reach for the task at hand. The lack of funds forced the firm to think frugally. So they made their own 360-degree system using projectors they adapted from regular ones used in classrooms, and made their dream of a festival simulator come true.

Tesla's game-changing Powerwall batteries enable homes and businesses to store solar energy and power from the grid, thus reducing electricity bills for the user by up to 25 per cent. These batteries are a classic example of frugal innovation from India.

*

Another famous example of frugal innovation from India, probably inspired by the fact that, in Indian villages, families of four are often seen squeezed onto a single scooter, is the Tata Nano, the world's cheapest family car.

In countries like India, frugal innovation is practised not only by conglomerates like Tata, but also by the common man, leading to life hacks which are rarely sophisticated in nature. In fact, sometimes they may just be quick and dirty DIY solutions. Sometimes they may even be breaking the law.

In this chapter I shall be referring to ideas that are ingenious in their simplicity and ease of implementation. I shall also refer more often to Indian examples than to those from the developed world in order to make a point about removing elitism from innovation.

Jugaad, or frugal innovation, is based on one simple rule: there is no rule. It's about doing whatever it takes to make things work your way. If the conventions do not permit this, change the conventions. If your audience does not approve of it, change your audience. If the cost is astronomical, do it on a shoestring.

The bottom line is, if the solution resonates with one individual it is bound to resonate with others. However, frugal innovation does not necessarily mean innovation that is cheap or of an inferior quality. It simply means finding a way to get the optimum efficiency by using materials economically, so that the solution or product is accessible to those it is intended for, both in terms of price as well as distribution.

*

Frugal innovation comes from nameless villagers in remote India often with no proper means of transport. That's why, from what I understand, Mr Anil Gupta, a professor at the Indian Institute of Management Ahmedabad (IIMA), travels around India on foot in order to find young people who have ideas but neither the funds nor the resources to get those ideas into the wider world.

Thanks to Mr Gupta's work such people are acknowledged for their inventions even though they have neither formal education nor a desire to be in the limelight.

Consider a non-stick Teflon pan. Let's say it costs about $10. Use it for a few months and the Teflon surface starts to come off. Although it's not meant to be eaten, bits of the surface will inevitably be consumed with meals. Now consider a non-stick pan made of clay, such as the one made by Mansukhbhai Prajapati. It costs less than a dollar. And, clay being a natural material, it works better than a Teflon-coated non-stick pan, and it does not end up in your stomach. So it's energy-efficient, healthier, better and much more affordable than Teflon. Additional proof that quality does not always have to come at a huge cost.

Another case in point: India does not have a healthcare insurance system provided by the government; most healthcare expenses are paid out of patients' pockets. It is the private sector players who dominate the healthcare industry in India, making quality health-care a very effective but also a very expensive affair. This naturally means that the poor in India need frugally innovative solutions to maintain their health.

It was important to give the hope of good cardiac care to billions of people who have comparatively weak hearts, as proven by numerous medical studies.* Cardiologist Dr Devi Shetty started running the Narayana Hrudayalaya Heart Hospital in Bangalore with one objective in mind: to remove the association of healthcare from affluence. In his hospital at least 600 open-heart surgeries are performed every week at one-tenth of the cost of an open-heart surgery performed in the United States. Yet the mortality rate thirty days after the surgery at Narayana Hrudayalaya Hospital is 1.27 per cent, and the infection rate for a coronary artery bypass graft procedure is 1 per cent, which is as good as that of US hospitals.

The cost of the entire procedure is one-tenth of that in the United States simply because Dr Shetty came up with a model that lever-aged economies of scale. He built large hospitals and attracted many poor patients through micro-insurance schemes, a kind of insurance plan meant to protect low-income households, by having them pay much lower premiums than regular insurance schemes.

If hospitals were run like no-frills airlines, for instance, or if air conditioning was limited to operating theatres or intensive care units, or if they were run like Walmart, leading to cheaper prices for expensive things like heart valves bought in bulk, we would have a frugally innovative model like Narayana Hrudayalaya

---

* Source: https://timesofindia.indiatimes.com/city/pune/Indians-more-prone-to-heart-diseases/articleshow/5060885.cms

Hospital. Once the doctors started adopting this model, they realised that as they operated on more patients, the results got better and the costs got lower.

It is possible to innovate under all circumstances, as in the case of Dr Devi Shetty, while being generous and philanthropic and still maintaining a sense of business.

On the night of 23 September 2014, India's Mars Orbiter Mission, also known as Mangalyaan, successfully entered the orbit of Mars. The mission cost $74 million. At the time, the Indian prime minister joked that the mission had cost less than making the movie *Gravity*, which cost $100 million.

India not only became the first country in the world to reach Mars at its first attempt but also spent the least amount of money to get there. But frugal innovations are not intended just for giving yourself a pat on the back for being resourceful; the Indian Space Research Organisation, or ISRO, also beams educational programmes and supervises surgeries in far-flung villages through telemedicine.

On one hand we have an ambitious and innovative space race brewing up; on the other, we have our folk in Punjab who make huge quantities of lassi, a deliciously thick yogurt drink, whipped up not in a regular blender, but in locally produced washing machines. The whipping action required for the lassi is perfectly suited to that of the washing machine. The large volume held by the washing machine also means it can cater for the large number of people it is meant to serve, especially during the harsh heat waves that frequently occur in Punjab.

Another example, this time in the sartorial world: in order to double the speed of their work, tailors in smaller Indian towns incorporate the measuring tape onto their scissors, so that they can cut pieces of cloth without having to measure them first. They can see at a glance exactly when they have to stop cutting.

And then there is a plethora of everyday examples, including sunglasses with built-in music players, the potato-powered digital clock and the chandelier made of plastic bottles.

When you reduce the number of resources you have to work with, you have to think differently. There is increasing evidence that limited resources and makeshift thinking can be scaled to Western markets and to the wider world.

Innovation need not always be extravagant. For instance, General Electric made a highly affordable ECG machine for the poor in India by cleverly cutting costs. Among other things, GE produced a small printer to print bus tickets, which made the ECG machine much more affordable. But this ECG machine did not just sell in India, it also sold in ninety other countries.

Speaking of democratising medical facilities, victims of accidents often cannot afford top-quality prosthetic limbs. One temple sculptor was frustrated by this, and went on to design and make prosthetic limbs from simple materials like wood and rubber. They are available for less than $45 and are worn by at least 20,000 people every year. Of course, they may not be the most advanced prosthetic limbs in the world but they allow amputees to run, sit cross-legged and even squat. This temple sculptor's Jugaad has led Stanford University and D-Rev to collaborate and develop a $20 prosthetic knee joint that can be assembled in less than an hour. In 2009 it was named by *Time* magazine as one of the fifty best inventions in the world, just another example of a liberating idea conceived under financial constraints, that has spread beyond the boundaries of India.

Innovation is possible for everyone – not just the privileged and the wealthy but also the poorest of the poor, the everyman, in every developing country. Countries like India, Brazil, China, Indonesia and Kenya.

From the local honey seller Mohammed Saidullah, who created an amphibious bicycle, to Mr Markani, who created a water-fuelled car, there are thousands of small-town innovators in India who are naturally inventive but not necessarily well educated.

Indeed, maybe it is this very lack of education that helps open minds towards new possibilities. Maybe an educated mind follows too many rules, and does not ask enough questions. But an uneducated mind is lateral, simple and ridiculously audacious.

Imagine the hidden creativity within so many people – people with ideas that may not change the world, but will bring about a change to *their* own world, which may be full of hardships and inconveniences.

The most important thing about Jugaad is that it thrives on chaos and uncertainty. India is probably the most chaotic country in the world: elephants blocking traffic; cow dung used as fuel; superstitious scientists; the power of mind over matter; more than a billion people screaming to get their voices heard in the world's largest democracy; spiritual and non-materialistic ideologies clashing with the ambition of the country to become an economic powerhouse; a rising number of small enterprises with a do or die approach to success despite all the red tape involved.

Common Indian wisdom has it that nothing in the world is constant. Hence Indians are comfortable with chaos and unpredictability, which suits their mindset of Jugaad just fine.

In the future India may continue to be disorganised for a while – a terrible thing for civilised existence as understood by the Western world perhaps – but an ideal way for looking at the world upside down and coming up with new ideas that make people's lives easier.

Perhaps within this hacker mentality, this impulse to fix problems on a daily basis, lies the potential for a country to fix larger, more global problems, to scale the solutions to a bigger target audience and finally make not just their own world, but the wider world, a better place.

TEACHER

INTRODUCTION

By Scott Morrison, Founder of the Boom!

'The illiterate of the twenty-first century won't be those who can't read or write. But those who can't learn, unlearn and relearn'
– Alvin Toffler

MY MATE READ HIS FIRST BOOK AT THE AGE OF THIRTY-SIX

He jokes that before then, *all* menus were Greek to him. The ATM was a one-armed bandit ('it always took my card and never gave me money'). He'd always seen himself as different, but he'd managed to hide his lack of reading skills well. Especially from his kids. He tells me that for years the stigma forced him to bury it deeper. Until, one day, he told himself he needed to learn to read.

LAST YEAR, HE WROTE AND READ HIS WEDDING VOWS

The prejudice and stigma attached to my friend's illiteracy and perceived lack of skill were enough to make him feel isolated, excluded and an outsider. But after years of ignoring it, he grabbed the bull by the horns and metaphorically kicked the shit out of the illiteracy demon so that he could experience the joys of a good story. In his words, 'what can be better than being let in on the secret of understanding?'

Coming into the twentieth century, around 79 per cent of the world's population was illiterate. *Seventy-nine per cent!* As we entered the millennium, that number had decreased massively to a respectable (but still too high) 18 per cent. Humanity's thirst for knowledge, our need to be sated by literature, content and social media, is driving the numbers down to the point where we'll talk of an inability to read and write as an anachronism, much as we do diphtheria and smallpox.

I'm massively chuffed for my mate – not least because he's promised to buy this book! – but it ignited my thinking for this chapter. It made me think about his determination and singular focus on the pen and the written word to overcome illiteracy as some kind of superpower. And, if that was a superpower to defeat the twentieth-century version of illiteracy, what would be needed to overcome its twenty-first century iteration?

It's the search for this superpower that has fascinated me for half a decade. And it's the point of this chapter.

Alvin Toffler was an American writer and futurist whose works predicted much of what is currently impacting culture and society right now despite being written back in 1970. He foresaw the digital and communication revolutions and his seminal work, *Future Shock*, seemed way out even for the era of glam rock and ganja but sets out a way of life we take for granted today. His prescience concerning the rental and gig economies and the impact of significant granularity on advertising made him seem at the time like some kind of reader of tea leaves at the local fairground. No longer: these are all real, impactful and powerful movements affecting how we do, run and engage with businesses. Not only that, they're shaping the way we build, manage and shift our careers. We are constantly flexing, learning or discarding what we consider to be the core skills needed to keep up with this ever-changing world.

If we are to avoid this new kind of illiteracy, to prevent ourselves becoming obsolete in Toffler's well-predicted vision of the twenty-first century, we need to hone our personal approach to always being able to update our own internal operating system. It's this new way that I want to explore in this section of the book – and it fundamentally involves turning our existing definition and expectation of what we call 'a teacher' on its head.

THE ROLE OF THE TEACHER

I'll get to the point. If I say to you 'geography teacher' you'll likely conjure up a picture in your head. I'll wager there are leather patches, cords and some gimpy glasses. And we're often rooted in that view of what the word 'teacher' means to us. Yes, we've all had a good teacher, one who pushed us really hard, helped us overcome our mountain of beans. But, for many of us, a teacher is someone who gave us information. Someone who 'taught' us. A kind of passive, 'needs must' rite of passage relationship. I pose a different question. What if you looked in the mirror and the teacher was

YOU. That there wasn't someone there to act as a teacher *for* you. Rather, the onus was solely *on* you to create your own path, your own way – to unleash the creative superpower of 'teacher'.

If preventing twentieth-century illiteracy was focused on us *being taught*, avoiding a similar fate in the twenty-first century involves us *teaching ourselves – and taking on board the concept of learning, unlearning and relearning*.

That's where I found myself about five years ago.

After twenty years of working in big global brands and ad agencies, I decided it was time to strike out on my own. I felt that I had learned so much, gained so much experience and delivered enough to be able to build a business from it. In a wave of naivety, I believed that what I had learned would be the thing that moved me into the next level. Big mistake.

Dr Carol Dweck's brilliant work[*] on fixed and growth mindsets makes a comfortable bedfellow in this new shift – fail to take the simple steps that will allow you to be open to new ideas, new thinking and learning and you'll suffer the same lack of under-standing as Victorian schoolchildren trying to extract meaning from a simple text.

Once I got my head around the marriage of Dweck and Toffler's philosophies, it became clear that there's a seismic cultural shift happening that their thinking underpins. That people in a wide

---

[*] Mindset: Changing The Way You think To Fulfil Your Potential

variety of sectors all over the world are rapidly upskilling themselves, unlearning and relearning the skills that they need to thrive in the global workplace. Digital nomads are trekking through Colombia for six months while coding for four hours a night, constantly changing their personal business models to get the most out of life. The number of people enrolling in online learning in countries like India is up 55 per cent year on year as they hungrily shed their old habits and learnings, to quickly anchor their relearning in new, profitable and globally tradable skills.

But this is only one angle. 'AI is collar blind,' comments Calum Chace, author of *The Economic Singularity*, supporting a series of reports that suggest by the mid-2030s between 38 and 47 per cent of jobs will be replaced by AI. Indeed, even by 2020, 50 per cent of the US workforce will be freelance (*Forbes*). This so-called 'liquid talent' doesn't look at the traditional models of boss as teacher or HR as gatekeeper to learning to help them learn and grow. They themselves are identifying areas where they can unlearn and relearn, transforming their skills and their lives from a reactive paradigm to a more proactive, constantly evolving learning approach. And because the world is becoming more comfortable with this, it is starting to impact how businesses shape their own approach to training and growing their team's capabilities. By the time the robots take their jobs, this breed of worker will have reskilled several times to become the human operating system on top of several layers of AI, bringing new ways for man and machine to work together.

*

With this exciting movement upon us, I wanted to use this section of the book to provide a blueprint, a set of approaches and some interesting points of view, that will help anyone wanting to shift this teaching paradigm for themselves to find a starting point. I wanted to share essays from people who have created the tools, philosophies and ways of being that can bring life to the creative superpower that is teacher.

THE PHILOSOPHY OF LEARNING BY DOING: David Erixon at Hyper Island

'For the things we have to learn before we can do them, we learn by doing them.'
— Aristotle

I remember the squeak of the spanner on the bolt as my dad removed my stabilisers. It wasn't an innocent, mouse-type squeak. It was the deafening screech indicating that I was about to do something I'd never done before. Riding a bike without stabilisers when you're four isn't the same as watching someone do it. Other kids flew round the playground with consummate ease. I, at the other extreme, was about to undergo a rite of passage that meant my life as a young boy would never be the same. I remember feeling my dad's steady hand behind me, falling off four times and crying at my lack of ability. On the fifth go, as I told him I was too scared, my dad pushed, let go and I flew (figuratively speaking, of course!).

Learning by doing is the most powerful way to embed knowledge. Acquiring it is one thing. We can read books, watch others and even take courses. However, as Benjamin Franklin sagely observed, 'Tell me and I forget. Teach me and I remember. Involve me and I learn.' Like riding a bike without stabilisers, the only way to successfully gain the skills required to step up in our careers, or learn to play an instrument of choice, for that matter, is by doing. When we're able to embrace this, we observe our own foibles, develop our strengths and identify areas of development more quickly.

In his chapter, David Erixon shares the philosophy of learning by doing as created at Hyper Island. Known around the world as the 'Digital Harvard', it was founded in 1996 and now has a presence in Sweden, Brazil, UK, the US and Singapore. Its core tenets revolve around experiential learning, lifelong learning and reflection and teamwork.

David's intriguing views on education, personal development and the power of learning in a different way, focused on real-life skills in real-life situations, is critical for people starting a business on their own. A framework and methodology for learning in the right way gives focus, impetus and scope for how to get the best out of yourself and bring to the fore your creative superpowers

UNLEARNING FROM THE STREETS: David Pearl, Street Wisdom

It was 8.35 on a cold November morning. Forty of us, all sorts, from MDs to actors to writers, stood outside a Soho coffee shop awaiting the opportunity to walk the streets of London to regain perspective on areas of our lives that we wanted to reconnect with and overcome blockages in. I have to admit, I thought at first that this was some 'Kum Ba Yar', loon-pantery thing I'd see at Glastonbury or Woodstock. It wasn't. It changed my life and two years later I became a director at one of the most incredible movements in the world – Street Wisdom.

We can become so disconnected from ourselves, from what we set out to do and the power that lives inside of us. Our superpowers become dulled and we are left with the same old knowledge that we desperately try to repurpose so as to get us to the next stage of our careers/lives. However, as Marshall Goldsmith so beautifully observed in the title of his bestselling book, 'what got you here won't get you there'. In his teachings, he helps people to reconnect with themselves and learn what they need to unlearn by doing things that feel really counter to your previous experiences. Give away ALL the credit (who knew!), create a to-stop doing list rather than a to-do list (what?) and question your flaws. All useful and great in essence, but how do you actually create a space for yourself to unlearn these things? How do you reconnect with yourself in a way that gets to the core of the questions you need to ask and understand what you need to relearn?

Enter Street Wisdom.

David Pearl's chapter shares how he created a wonderfully simple framework for asking these types of questions and getting the answers you seek by using something we venture down each day as a teacher: the street. By following the four-stage plan that David created, countless people have found answers to deep questions that have prevented them from progressing and getting 'there' (wherever 'there' might be). It's had a profound impact on how people reconnect with themselves and find a way to channel their inner creative superpowers to come out with a clearer way forward. Simply put, the street, your subconscious and the willingness to try something different will help you unlearn and set you up to relearn with power and precision. By shifting our perspective on something we take for granted each day, we allow the street to become an ally in helping teach ourselves the skill of unlearning.

LEARNING IN REVERSE: Nadya Powell, Utopia

'Pencil to the left, pointing upwards towards the top of the notepad. Tea and coffee delivered five minutes before the meeting and you get up and serve it to each client. Biscuit refresh every half an hour.'

Being a grad back in the day had some very specific rules. Aside from being in charge of refreshments, there were reports to write, faxes to send and egos to massage. Your opinion on the client's go-to-market strategy was far less important than your ability to book a table in Soho within thirty minutes. This doesn't wash anymore. The younger generation have more to say, more experience and a far more forthright view on where they see they add value than ever before. And it's not by passing the custard creams.

Nadya's chapter challenges the old-world view of teacher and pupil in business. The expectation that the 'higher ups' have all the answers and knowledge is no longer applicable and is frankly counter to creating a culture where creative superpowers can flourish.

Relearning from the youngest people in the business is a powerful way to stay relevant, get fresh perspectives and build highly motivated teams who aren't afraid to experiment. I conducted research with fifty CMOs (chief marketing officers) around the world, 75 per cent of whom told us that getting young talent into their business when they could work at Google or Facebook was one of their biggest challenges. With that in mind, organisations will need to relearn how they work with young talent to make their businesses places where they want to come, add value and stay. Nadya's perspective on this is built from her own experience and, as she notes, it has given her an opportunity to build and unleash creative superpowers across the business.

WHAT'S AT THE HEART OF THIS CREATIVE SUPERPOWER?

My final thought about actively engaging in a shift to teaching oneself is this. We often hear the phrase 'fail fast' – it's de rigueur and feels great to announce it to the business. Except often our teams or shareholders don't really want to believe it. Failing = making a big mistake = losing your job = losing your home = no thanks. It's time to reframe that in the context of this chapter. The most powerful articulation of it for me is not to 'fail fast' but to 'learn, unlearn and relearn fast'. It's a mouthful and not quite as pithy a comment to put on your business's latest job spec. However, the reality is that when you ask people what their key motivation for coming to work is, what gets them out of bed in the morning, it's the idea that they come to work to learn and develop; conversely, inertia is often quoted as the most common reason for leaving.

So isn't it time that we put learning, unlearning and relearning at the heart of our culture? That way, people are free to connect with themselves, understand what they need to do to become better and relearn those skills, often by doing them in the role. It allows people to 'fail' because that's simply part of unlearning and relearning. It's also a much more powerful call to action to young talent as it's how they live their lives – they don't want to be taught by teachers, they want to actively learn through experimentation and share that to make where they work better.

We are now empowered more than at any other time to leverage the creative superpower of teacher. Recognising that there's an enormous emphasis and opportunity for us to *be the teacher for ourselves* as opposed to *waiting to be taught* is empowering people all over the world to become highly skilled, flexible and creative global business leaders. What fuels the superpower are the philosophies of Dweck's growth mindset and Toffler's learn, unlearn and relearn. Combined, they will unblock, unlock and unleash you and your team's ability to be more creative, keeping you sharp, hungry and fundamentally . . .

. . . one of the twenty-first-century literate.

DOING-BY-LEARNING

By David Erixon, Co-founder of Hyper Island

It seems that we keep coming back to a paradigm shift that is happening in the way we create, produce, consume and communicate; and, equally, how we destroy and unsustain the world we are sharing. The human condition makes change hard for us to accept while institutional forces make any disruption arising from change hard to maintain. We have to continuously create and learn not to stay still. This is a challenge for traditional educational systems – and organisational models built on a factory mentality – since they seem to leave us ill-equipped to handle disruption while the 'war stories' of success taught in business schools and workplaces reinforce a sense that there is a singular endgame rather than an ever-changing journey.

This chapter is not about the future *what* of business. It is, however, about *how* we might get there. As creators (and, equally, destroyers; such are the dynamics of business) we are inevitably faced with the necessity to rethink and redo the way we create customers and grow new markets as the old ways are either no longer serving us or are simply not working. Not only do we need to let go of the current system from which we operate, which in itself is difficult – so much of our modus operandi is habitual and incremental and this is a comfort zone from which we operate most of the time – we also need to create and jump to entirely new ones. In many ways this is a jump into an unformed unknown. Learning, I would argue, done in the right way, is the key for doing this successfully. Learning as the way to transform how we do business.

EXPERIMENTING WITH LEARNING-BY-DOING AND EXPERIENTIAL LEARNING AT HYPER ISLAND

Hyper Island, a tertiary-level school I co-founded in 1995, has become synonymous with learning-by-doing, a type of learning process focused on *experiencing* as a way for participants to acquire and expand knowledge in a constantly changing environment.

When Hyper Island was founded our mission was to teach people about things that at the time we knew very little about. We had to find both a practice and a metaphysical concept of learning that would allow us to create an education for, and somewhat from, the future. It wasn't enough for us to teach people how to fish, to paraphrase an old saying; we wanted to teach people how to learn in an accelerated way. Our answer: learning-by-doing, a learning process derived from the concept of pragmatism; an experiential, or experience-based, approach to learning.

Most people mistakenly think that learning-by-doing is a 'trial and error' activity, almost mechanical, focused on a certain practice of an individual – do, do and do again, until you get it right – and that it is merely used for learning in a causal container of 'if then', a test environment for inferred mental or physical schemes. It would mean that we can only test things that have already been proven (or for which there is a set rulebook), and, therefore, we can only learn what is already known (or defined by set forces; think determinism). It would be a substandard methodology for venturing into the unknown; it would simply not know how to deal with it, apart from trying to fit things into an existing scheme.

Nothing could be further from the essence of learning-by-doing. Learning-by-doing is a term that would perhaps be better explained by *learning through reflection on, and while, doing*. At the heart of this approach sits the human experience, where *experience* is both the process of experiencing and the result of the process. It's in the actual transactions between people and their environments that difficulties emerge, and it is with experience that problems and opportunities are resolved or explored through questioning and inquiry. Critical and reflective thinking is also key to this process (although some people unfortunately decouple 'critical' from 'thinking'; and some misinterpret 'critical' as 'negative'), and so is playful and imaginative thinking. Learning-by-doing doesn't separate thinking from doing, in fact it brings the two together. It contains the anticipatory inquiry into 'what if' and it is inherently trying out the unknown, using the whole person (sensing, thinking, feeling, intuiting, imagining, acting, etc.), preferably within a larger collective context where ideas can be multi-dimensionalised and used to allow new patterns to emerge.

*

At Hyper Island we refer to this ongoing process as the learning spiral. It's an adaptation of David Kolb's Learning Cycle: Concrete Experience → Reflective Observation → Abstract Conceptualisation → Active Experimentation, but it also includes people and our environments: The Life World (a combination of the whole person – body, mind, self, life history, etc.), the context of learning (why, how, what, and with whom we are learning), as well as the awareness of the changes that are taking place. As we move through this spiral we observe changes and we are deliberate about experiencing and affirming our own (and others') experience, which generates growth and change.

Consequently, we must not take the person out of the learning equation (which most education does). The self is a rich instrument, which is why self-awareness is key.

You have to include yourself fully in the learning process if you want to create from another level of consciousness (outside the habitual patterns). Repeat, refer and review are levels of learning that require very little personal responsibility or contribution. The level of learning we aim for is reflection (which is where meaning originates) and for that the self has to be included (an open exploration of beliefs, actions, feelings, identity, etc.) in order to bring home learning fully. Ultimately, this is the level from which we create with insight and will.

DIFFERENT TYPES OF LEARNING CHALLENGES REQUIRE DIFFERENT TYPES OF LEARNING METHODS

Most learning that takes place in our everyday lives is assimilative. It means that we have an existing set of beliefs of the world and how it works and all we are doing-while-learning is adding to that pattern – usually with small, incremental changes or refinements. We are learning-by-adding to that which already exists. This is usually what happens in a classroom – or a boardroom – where a subject is built up by means of constant additions to what has already been learned.

If the world was changing incrementally, assimilative learning methods would be relevant as a way to cope with that change (and so would incremental innovation as a way to make what is there a little bit better). Those practices that are occupied with entirely new patterns are described as accommodative or transcendent. This type of learning contains the destruction of existing patterns: how to deconstruct, unlearn and ultimately destroy no longer productive beliefs and the transformation of mental, sometimes even physical, schemes. We have to relinquish and reconstruct the world, and this can be experienced as very demanding, sometimes even painful. Most patterns, schemes or paradigms also include ideas of our own identity. When those patterns change, so does our own idea of ourselves. This is why some learning experience has to be transformational of the self, of our being, in order to be constructive in what's emerging; to thrive in a new present time.

Learning-by-doing staged and facilitated in the right way, enables these transformations to happen, both faster and easier for the individual to cope with. It's a myth that change has to be painful – this, after all, is just another belief. Through learning-by-doing participants are constantly working with their own experiences, and they are given the tools to explore it, be aware of it, look at it without judgement, and play with options. What if?

A LEARNING ENVIRONMENT, A COLLECTIVE PURSUIT

Another aspect of learning-by-doing is the emphasis it puts on the environment and the social context of the learning. This includes the importance of communities of practice (a term coined by Etienne Wenger, a Swiss educational theorist and practitioner) to describe the role of communities in learning and how the social context of our selves impacts our ability to learn. In Wenger's research of communities of practice he shows that most learning does not take place together with the expert, but among the apprentices. This suggests that learning is a social technology within a community of practitioners, practised daily.

At Hyper Island, we place more emphasis on generating and supporting the right environment for accommodative learning to emerge within a group of participants, then time spent with particular individuals within that group. This is also why we care more about facilitation than the teacher or the master in the classroom. Culture is a powerful thing. Effective membership – including such human phenomena as belonging and inclusion – mutuality, shared purpose, shared values, cooperation and peer-to-peer support, are far greater levers for delivering powerful learning experiences than just the 'inner environment' of an individual.

Compare this with a traditional classroom where most work is individual and where individuals are 'shielded' from the group, premiering individual achievements, creating competition within the classroom through a Bell curve distribution of grades and rewards. This is also how most workplaces are organised and led.

Now, think of your own workplace and how it's set up to learn from the future. Then ask yourself how to support people on their transformational learning quests. Would you send someone on a course, or would you change the environment in which the person works. Perhaps both? I think a good analogy would be a sick fish in a toxic fish tank – would you give the fish some drugs, or would you change the water in the tank? (Again, perhaps both: there is a short-term and a long-term aspect to it.)

MINDSET AND LANGUAGE

The final aspect of learning-by-doing is the importance of identifying the form that is being transformed. Metaphorically it's about establishing your starting point, the current paradigm or pattern that you are locked into. It's what Mezirow referred to as frame of reference. This process is closely related to language. Transformational learning is always to some extent an epistemological change rather than merely a change in behavioural repertoire or an increase in the quantity or fund of knowledge. In other words, the learning process needs to support the creation of new language in order to reflect new ideas. It is the creation of memes we're dealing with here. Knowledge as strings of thought, punctuating existing notions, becoming part of the foundation of new ones; shaping our future experiences. Or, as Wittgenstein put it: 'The limits of my language are the limits of my world.'

This is, in my experience, the trickiest part of the learning process. The production of language requires some specific talents which take great effort to acquire – or skills by a facilitator to unleash. Language is perhaps the most powerful tool of creation.

> *'In the beginning was the Word, and the Word was with God, and the Word was God.'*   – John 1:1

DOING-BY-LEARNING VS LEARNING-BY-DOING

This brings me to the title of this essay, 'Doing-by-Learning', a subtle remark up to this point but an important one hereafter.

Most education seems to consider 'learning' to be the end goal, rather than a means to an end. We go to school to learn, and, even at Hyper Island, we talk about learning-by-doing as if doing was just another way in which to learn, instead of the other way around.

Focusing on the learning as a means to an end is an interesting starting point for the future of learning. It's already reflected in cultural phenomena such as the makers movement, various platforms for co-creation, manifested in participatory events such as burns. Audacious dreams and visions, followed by energetic exploration – and learning – in the pursuit of making those dreams a reality. The act of manifesting creation becomes the event which fuels the spiral of learning.

Perhaps this is the real problem of business today, and why, perhaps, business has not already been reinvented for this era of unknowns. It seems as if business leaders have lost the ability to envisage an alternative future. Lost the ability to create. And that's why we are not learning more, or faster. The key ability is to dream audaciously and be visionary in your creative pursuits. The rest is actually just doing-by-learning.

If you're interested in exploring this for your own professional environment, I suggest the following inroads:

1. Identify your 'business of the unknown', i.e. what part of your business will you have to radically recreate over the next few years, either for survival or for growth opportunity. This will be your purpose and motivation for doing things differently.

2. Make the deliberate decision that doing-by-learning will be your strategy for how to make the unknown your future business.

3. Establish a solid understanding of this approach (and do it by experiencing it as opposed to reading about it in a book, although those are obviously not mutually exclusive).

4. Find the people in your organisation who are up for it (and they can be anywhere, even in Reception), connect them, make them a network.

5. When you have established this community, turn it into a learning community and find ways of doing this that is sustainable (personally I'm a big fan of Agile as it has got learning at its core, but there are many methods out there. Find the one that suits you and your needs).

6. Focus this learning community on creating the future (using learning as the way to do it).

7. Create new rituals and use (new) language to expand the power of that learning.

8. Turn every failure, problem, challenge, negative thought, discouragement into an opportunity (and read up on appreciative inquiry).

9. Keep bringing it back to what needs to be created and, as a consequence, what you need to learn, and how.

10. Notice all changes, even the smallest, and celebrate the shit out of them.

STREET WISDOM: ANSWERS ARE EVERYWHERE

By David Pearl, Founder of Street Wisdom

A NEW SCHOOL OF THE STREETS

'People usually consider walking on water or in thin air a miracle. But I think the real miracle is not to walk either on water or in thin air, but to walk on earth. Every day we are engaged in a miracle which we don't even recognise.'

– Thich Nhat Hanh

'I'VE NEVER BEEN FOR A WALK . . .'

A young woman has just stood up at the end of a Street Wisdom event we are running for a giant electronics retailer. She has tears in her eyes. She's one of 250 store managers the company has gathered from all over the UK to think fresh about the customer experience. Retail is a competitive business. It can also be a repetitive one. If you're not careful, one customer can start looking like every other one and shopping can become purely transactional. So these hard-working sales people have been taken out of their daily surroundings and we've just placed them in another environment, one which they wouldn't normally associate with learning – the street. And now, having gone through a Street Wisdom experience this young woman has something to say.

'I have never been for a walk . . .'

You can hear a pin drop. She goes on to explain. She's a doer, constantly busy, on her way from A to B. The street isn't a place to dwell, it's just the space between one task and another, something to be got through as quickly as possible. The Street Wisdom experience she has just had made her realise that she's never allowed herself to wander. To look around and take inspiration from the environment. To see the people around her as people, not just obstacles to avoid or customers to service. And it's a pattern she wants to relearn so she can enjoy life and connect with the world – and the people – around her in new ways.

Street Wisdom is an immersive three-hour workshop which takes the most everyday space we know – the Street – and turns it into a place where you can unlearn habitual thinking so you get fresh inspiration, solution, ideas and direction.

At the time of writing it's in thirty countries around the world. That's way beyond what I thought was possible the day I dreamed up Street Wisdom.

'WALKING IN CIRCLES'

It's spring 2012. I am in Amsterdam and, no surprise, it's raining. I am on Westerstraat, a broad, sweeping boulevard that's home to a bustling market, great cafés and some wonderful indie shops. But that's not where my attention is at present. I am focusing on my feet. And these feet seem to be taking me round and round in circles.

I had come to Westerstraat with a question in mind: 'where do I go next in my career?' It's something I think about often given that my working life has tended to unfold in unexpected ways (opera first, then theatre, advertising, TV and more theatre, then working with businesses on creativity and in parallel setting up an improv opera company, then moving to Italy and learning to fly and, and, and . . .). Instead of asking my friends, family, colleagues or consultants about my next career step, I thought I'd ask – the street.

Not the people in the street. But the street itself.

I'd spent the morning wandering up and down Westerstraat, tuning up my senses so I could see, hear and feel much more than I normally would as a tourist. I wanted to communicate with the environment, not just observe it. Sure, I'd had a few odd looks, though, as this is Amsterdam, fewer than you might expect in a less tolerant city. In fact, one of the things I had quickly learned is that most of the discomfort of *looking weird* was actually in my own head. People went on with their own business as I drifted in and out of shops, up and down the street, asking my question.

And now the street was answering in a way I could not ignore.

It felt as if I was in some force field that was keeping me rotating around the same small spot of pavement. As the Amsterdammers politely found their way around this gyrating Englishman, I realised the street was telling me 'stay with this – stay with this – don't rush off to the next thing – stay where you are and explore'.

I didn't know it then, but I had just taken a big step – a leap, in fact – towards setting up the non-profit, street-based learning movement I co-founded in 2013 with friend and fellow corporate mischief-maker Chris Baréz-Brown.

Looking back, the Street Wisdom story had actually started long before Amsterdam. One of the earliest, most powerful and shocking lessons I learned as a child was taught to me on the street. When I was nine, my kid brother was hit by a stolen car while I was walking him to school. My brother recovered: he is now a happy, successful lawyer and family guy. But reality never did. What I learned on that unforgettable, life-changing morning was that reality isn't what adults tell you it is. It's not some fixed, solid truth. It can be turned on its head in a second. Turned either way. From great to awful – as on that shocking morning. But also the other way – from dull to magical. Ever since I have been curious about what is going on under the surface of reality, about why we settle for dull day-to-day routine when the extraordinary is available at every moment. That's probably why, in recent years, I have chosen to spend a lot of time in places that my arts friends would think of as dull – offices, boardrooms, meetings – hunting out the magic that's there and which working people are usually too busy to notice, access or enjoy.

I have worked with some of the world's biggest and supposedly hard-nosed companies, helping them make their businesses (and working lives) more inspired and inspiring. I say *supposedly* because under the corporate veneer most people are just . . . people. And you really notice this the moment you take a client out of the office for a creative walk-and-talk. And I like to do this a lot. As you step through the revolving doors out into the street, *professionals* change back into *people*. There's something about our workplaces that imposes an identity on us. Out in the street no one knows or cares who you are, which is very liberating.

And it got me thinking.

'WHY NOT USE THE STREET TO LEARN?'

What if, instead of hurrying through the streets, heads down, headphones blaring, screening out the environment and locked in private worries, we started turning our attention outwards? What if we really connected with the world around us and asked it the questions we are trying to figure out in our own minds?

It's a new application of an age-old idea.

It's long been known that walking stimulates thinking. 'All truly great thoughts are conceived by walking,' said Nietzsche. 'My mind works only with my legs,' agreed Rousseau. The brain seems to mirror the body. When we stand up from the office desk and go for a walk, our thinking loosens up. The Eureka moment rarely happens sitting still, staring at a computer screen.

*

Nor is this the first time people have thought about using the urban landscape for inspiration. As the Industrial Revolution swept through nineteenth-century France a group of poets, philosophers and artists took to the city streets for inspiration. Rather than head into nature, the Flâneurs (strollers), as they called themselves, were entranced by stimulus available on the bustling pavement. As Baudelaire put it: 'You enter into the crowd as though it were an immense reservoir of electrical energy.'

Street Wisdom aims to weave these two elements together and offer the chance to transform the act of urban wandering into a learning experience: a school of the streets.

Think about the words way, path, course and curriculum. They each use the metaphor of a physical passage to describe the education process. With Street Wisdom we are just taking the connection more literally – provoking the urban public to think of the street not just as a means of getting from A to B, but as a learning zone.

Also, at a time when formal education is becoming prohibitively expensive, we wanted to create a radically simple way of learning that was universally accessible and *free*. An 'invisible university' of the streets where, as we like to say, *you don't pay fees, you pay attention*.

'THE CITY IS A STONE BOOK . . .'

So, how does the learning and, indeed, the *un*learning work?

It's a three-phase process which starts with a sequence of short, guided strolls designed to tune up your senses. This is essential for the second phase – the quest – where participants go for a longer walk and ask a question they want to answer before gathering together again in the third phase to share what they've learned. With heightened awareness – attention turned 'outwards' – the environment becomes a rich source of mental stimulus. Sounds, smells, overheard conversations, street signs, adverts, even discarded rubbish . . . anything and everything in a street can provoke new associations, jolt unexpected insight, fire fresh neural pathways in the mind. Especially when you have the intention of learning something – that's the reason we engineer asking a specific question into what might otherwise be a delightful but not very productive process.

We like to think of it as logging into the wisdom that's all around us and then hitting the search button. Or, as consultant Chris Malings put it nicely when he returned from his Street Wisdom experience, 'the city is a stone book'.

So what do people learn?

On their Street Wisdom quests, people have resolved problems dogging them for years, found new business ideas, reset direction, changed careers, learned how to deal differently with life and love, debts and death.

Questions on recent events I have personally led included:
  – where should I buy a new house?

– how can I solve a problem at work?
– how can I have more fun?
– what new product could I invent?
– how can I turn my hobby into a business?
– how can I make more friends?

We discourage questions that are too universal ('what is the meaning of life?') or too mundane ('should I move the washing machine?') but, outside those confines, pretty much anything goes.

And while the range of answers is as diverse as the participants themselves, common agreement does seem to be emerging about why people around the world find this disruptive form of education appealing.

'THE STREET IS AN INVISIBLE UNIVERSITY'

Street Wisdom turns mental fretting outwards and enrols the world around us in helping us solve our internal puzzles. We could have designed Street Wisdom without the quest phase – purely as a mindfulness exercise. The question was a deliberate addition, a way of applying mindfulness to useful outcome and to engage that part of our (mostly Western) mind that won't give us permission to take time off unless it's for a practical reason. In this sense, it's applied mindfulness, a mindful 'app'.

'I CAN CONVERT LOST TIME INTO LEARNING'

Most of us spend a significant amount of time travelling between home and work. And spend is the right word – it's an investment of time – but one where we are getting very little return. Street Wisdom techniques allow you to tune into the environment for insight anytime, anywhere. Even a five-minute walk can deliver new learning. Answers are everywhere you go. Every stranger you pass is a potential teacher.

'IT'S ON MY DOORSTEP'

It's become standard to think that inspiration is somewhere 'out there'. You need to hop on a plane and travel halfway around the world to get peace of mind, discover a new perspective and generally 'find yourself'. Street Wisdom shows you can find the miraculous on your doorstep if you want to. Cities are where we increasingly live, so it makes sense to tap into the knowledge that's right under our feet.

'I GET PERMISSION TO WANDER'

Street Wisdom encourages participants to wander. Not to take the most direct route, but the most interesting. 'Let's get lost and find lunch' is a favourite saying of Richard Bandler, the inventor of NLP. It's an invitation for the mind to stop working down habitual, well-trodden neural pathways and instead make serendipitous, creative new connections. To *un*learn what it knows and make space for new knowing.

Wandering can seem at first glance like wasting time. A mechanism like Street Wisdom gives purpose to what our busy brains would otherwise dismiss as purposeless. Actually, the people who need to give us permission to wander are ourselves.

Like the woman in the seminar we need to *un*learn the idea that walking is just about getting from A to B, and next time we have a question go and find one in the street.

Answers are everywhere.

LEARNING IN REVERSE

By Nadya Powell, Co-founder of Utopia

'Let your youth have free rein. It won't come again, so be bold,
and no repenting.'
                                                    – Nikos Kazantzakis

Picture the scene. Eight people are sitting around a meeting-room table discussing an interesting problem to solve. Each person brings something different to the discussion: one individual is embedded in popular culture; another is digitally savvy; another a demon with a timing plan.

You could be fooled into thinking this is the perfect business scenario but you would be wrong, for underneath lurks an unspoken inequality. Despite each member of the team making an equal contribution and working equal hours with equal responsibility, half the team are paid just a quarter of the other half's salary.

Why the 4:1 differential? Age. In the creative industries today there is a shocking reality: the young are frequently paid a quarter of the older person's salary simply because they've been alive for slightly less time.

*

Incorrect, I hear you cry – it's not age, it's EXPERIENCE that dictates, rightly, the differential. The older employees have seen more, heard more, done more. I'm sorry to break this to you but the vast majority of business experience gained over previous decades is no longer of value. Today the young have more of a sense of what drives business success than the old do.

If we want to continue to learn and develop, we need to let the young teach.

YOUNGER, WISER

The phrase *older and wiser* was once undoubtedly true. Today we should reverse this saying and adhere to the mantra *younger and wiser* – listening and learning from the youngest person in the room. Why? Because in the past two decades the world has fundamentally changed.

1. THE AGE OF KNOWLEDGE IRRELEVANCE

The term creative destruction was coined by economist Joseph Schumpeter to refer to the non-stop economic upheaval the world must go through to survive. It is even more salient today as creative destruction has sped up thanks to the never-ending rise of the digital economy, as eloquently described by Peter Drucker in the *Harvard Business Review*:[*]

> . . . *this means every organization has to prepare for the abandonment of everything it does. Managers have to learn to*

---

[*] The New Society of Organizations

ask every few years of every process, every product, every
procedure, every policy: 'If we did not do this already, would we
go into it now knowing what we now know?' If the answer is
no, the organization has to ask, 'So what do we do now?' And
it has to do something, and not say, 'Let's make another study.'

Undoubtedly we are experiencing an era of change like never before, with the fundamentals of business being challenged. Whereas previously you either worked in the public or private sector, the fastest growing sector is the self-employed, making up 16 per cent of the workforce in the UK.[*] The start-up economy has boomed with little sign of bust, and the number of start-ups has increased from 281,000 in 2007 to 657,790 in 2016.[†] A job for life is now something that has been consigned to history, with the average UK employee changing jobs ten to twelve times in their career.[‡] And we have seen businesses rise and fall like no other time in history, with average tenure on the Fortune 500 being reduced from sixty-one to eighteen years before they disappear altogether.[§]

The result of the upheaval is that what we knew to be true even two to three years ago is no longer relevant today. According to the World Economic Forum, Future of Jobs report, 50 per cent of

---

[*] *Daily Telegraph*, 18 January 2016, http://www.telegraph.co.uk/finance/jobs/12106318/The-self-employed-will-overtake-the-public-sector-with-the-gig-economy.html

[†] Centre for Entrepreneurs, press release, January 2017, https://centreforentrepreneurs.org/cfe-releases/2016-breaks-business-formation-records/?mc_cid=cd53b7970a&mc_eid=0804ec0dee

[‡] *Balance Magazine*, May 2017, https://www.thebalance.com/how-often-do-people-change-jobs-2060467

[§] Innosight article, January 2012, https://www.innosight.com/insight/creative-destruction-whips-through-corporate-america-an-innosight-executive-briefing-on-corporate-strategy/

subject knowledge acquired during the first year of a four-year technical degree is out of date by the time students graduate.[*]

Having historical experience is no longer of value as the world of business is being destroyed and rewritten every few years, and this impacts everything we touch. In 2015, just two years before the time of writing, I wrote a strategy for a business on how to leverage digital media for their brand. This document has no value today.

2. THE AGE OF OUTSOURCED KNOWLEDGE

In 2016, Tom Goodwin wrote in the magazine *GQ* a critique of the British education system and questioned whether its very purpose – instilling knowledge – has any relevance today: 'Do we even need knowledge in a world of Alexa and Siri? Is the skill of agility now more valuable than the gaining of knowledge?'

He is right; with just one tap of a finger knowledge is immediately accessible, enabling us to outsource our memories to, to name a few, Wikipedia, Google, and Twitter. Which means the human brain can stop trying to retain knowledge and instead get on with the business of being creative.

Of course, it's not just knowledge that can be accessed immediately online; experiences can also be shared and absorbed. Blogs, forums, Reddit and Quora all mean there are countless opportunities to have a conversation with someone and assimilate the

---

[*] World Economic Forum, The Future of Jobs, http://reports.weforum.org/future-of-jobs-2016/

knowledge they have previously gained. Taking time to learn and assemble knowledge, the benefit of age, is no longer required. You can simply ask for the information and it is there.

3. THE AGE WHERE LEARNING IS KING

In 2006 Oxford University* published a study demonstrating that the old saying 'You can't teach an old dog new tricks' is scientifically true as it showed the young find learning easier than the old. In 2016 Columbia University† published a study in the same vein seeking to understand the teenage brain and found teenagers have an innate ability to learn that outstrips the old, as summarised by Dr Shohamy: 'By connecting two things that aren't intrinsically connected, the adolescent brain may be trying to build a richer understanding of its surroundings during an important stage in life.'

These findings perhaps come as no surprise; the ability of the young to learn faster than the old is ingrained in the cultural norms of society. And we've experienced examples of this every day; try to teach Gran to conceive of let alone use Alexa and it may take some time. Introduce Alexa to a seven-year-old and their bond is immediate and almost natural.

But we're missing the point – the ability to learn faster changes everything. In the age of creative destruction, where what was relevant a year ago is no longer relevant today, the ability to learn

---

* BBC News report, 2006, http://news.bbc.co.uk/1/hi/health/6172048.stm
† Zuckerman Institute report, 2016, https://zuckermaninstitute.columbia.edu/brain-study-reveals-how-teens-learn-differently-adults

is critical to survival and it delivers a huge advantage to the young.

And the reality is that the young have grown up in the age of creative disruption and thrive within it. Gen Y grew up with stability, structure and hierarchy, where employment was certain and for life and struggle with the constant change and relearning the current disruptive culture demands. The young, however, were designed for the new world economy, knowing no different and often leading the way.

Experience has less value, knowledge is immediate and the young are able to adapt and learn, striding through the age of creative destruction. Change will keep occurring so the more adaptable and flexible you are, the fitter you will be for the future. The saying 'older, wiser' no longer makes sense; 'younger, wiser' is now more apt. Why spend time listening to your boss when you can learn more from the intern?

YOUNGER AND OLDER, WISER

Let's pause for a breather. Being 'old' myself, I would suggest we do have some value. The old can teach us how to handle that most tricky of animals – human beings.

No matter the volume of online material you read, or new technologies you adopt, learning emotional intelligence, how to influence people, how to cope with the many vagaries of humankind, takes both time and experience. When sitting in a difficult meeting with your boss, your colleague, or your client, knowing what to say, and when and how to say it, is a deeply learned skill.

On many occasions, for example, I've observed a brilliant twenty-five-year-old, whose ideas far outweigh mine for brilliance, struggle to explain the idea, sell the idea and bring the team along on the journey. Humans take time to understand and, as the old have spent that time, they excel at this.

The young have relevance, the old the ability to influence. Knowledge and experience are equal for both; 'younger and older, wiser' is the refrain to repeat. To get the benefit of their diverse perspectives the most important thing is to enable both to have an equal voice in the room.

LET THEM TEACH!

Society, business and culture are constructed in such a way as to make it almost impossible for the young to leverage the positive impact they can have. The older, experienced boss gets more time in the room. The older, experienced client gets to make the final call.

We need to re-evaluate some of the deepest foundations of business and be prepared to rip them out and build new ones. We need to change how business is done to enable the young to teach and the old to learn.

*

Here are three ways to empower the young and future-proof your business, all shaped by conversations with leaders, my own experiences and the vital opinions of the young.

1. CHANGE YOUR ORGANISATIONAL STRUCTURE

Business is typically structured hierarchically according to experience, and therefore age. This structure smothers voices as it is predicated on the older and more 'experienced' voices having more value than the younger. To enable the young to teach, consider a model that replaces a hierarchical team with a flatter structure.

One example of this is holacracy. This practice recommends the removal of hierarchical pyramid structures, replacing them with non-hierarchical clusters of individuals, called circles, organised around the project in hand. Doing this not only delivers greater agility and encourages collaboration but it also flattens out businesses, thereby enabling more voices, especially the younger, to be heard. You can read all about it at http://www.holacracy.org/.

Job roles and titles should also be reconsidered. Typically, job roles are organised around fixed tiers of seniority with the assumption that the more years in service someone has the more senior a role they are relevant for. Remove the predication on experience and consider creating leapable structures. Leapable structures enable individuals to move from department to department or role to role, fast-tracking their experience and removing the barrier of age. This provides individuals with a portfolio of immediate and relevant experiences that will teach and empower everyone.

*

Institute millennial mentoring, a form of reverse mentoring, whereby the young mentor the old on new and modern ways of doing business. When combined with the CEO's influencer skills, the youngs' ability to adapt and assimilate the new will create a powerful combination.

Most importantly, if you want to keep the young within your business you need to remove the slow crawl up the professional ladder, and instead burn it. Chillingly, why would anyone put themselves through a tedious procession of job roles when they can build a business on YouTube or start a business with TechStars?

2. CHANGE HOW YOU MANAGE YOUNG TALENT

One of the more frequent complaints about the millennial generation is their sense of entitlement. This is false – millennials grew up with a style of parenting where they got a say in key decisions and, guess what, they rightly bring that attitude to work with them. They also grew up in a world where work does not mean 'desk' and job does not mean 'employee'. To ensure the young succeed and prosper we must create an environment that is tailored to their specific needs.

Support portfolio careers and allow the young (and old!) to work for both your business and another. Encourage them to investigate start-up opportunities, to assist someone they admire, to look outside the corporate walls. This duality of professional experience will benefit both businesses and the loyalty you will get in return will be transformative.

*

Remove any bias you have to encouraging digital nomadism – allow anyone to work from anywhere. If your team want to take a month to work from Bolivia, within reason, allow it. Once again, this experience will teach both of you so much about different ways to do business as well as the world of remote working technology. Experiment. You might like it.

Change your perception of leadership from one of 'lead from the front' to 'active enablement'. If you're a leader, when next in a meeting don't state your point of view first; instead, ask the youngest person in the room for their opinion and actively listen without prejudice. If they struggle to articulate themselves, be patient and give them time and room to explain. Diversity of opinion and thought is central to business success, and embracing the young critical.

3. CHANGE REMUNERATION MODELS

Time to revisit the 4:1 salary situation mentioned at the beginning of the chapter. For a person to want to offer an opinion, they need to feel it is of value, yet if the remuneration model a business employs is based on the outmoded view that older equals wiser, and they are paid as such, this won't occur.

Let's get really brave. Consider this: pay every member of staff exactly the same wage. Decide upon the amount by taking the mean average of all salaries currently being paid and then apply it to everyone. To create necessary pay differentials, construct a reward system based on value given to the business, not whether someone has a senior title or not.

*

Then put the icing on the cake; make like John Lewis and implement an employee stock ownership plan (ESOP), ensuring everyone has a stake in the success or failure of the enterprise.

Deep breath.

By demonstrating you believe the young have value, you will get value back in the form of new opinions and experiences. You will learn things you never knew existed until that moment you changed and started to listen.

TOGETHER, SURVIVING CREATIVE DESTRUCTION

Hopefully you will now look at the young person in the room as the sage, not the opinionated upstart. We all want to learn, and, by changing how we structure our organisations and empower and reward our young talent, a new set of teachers will emerge who want nothing more than to have a positive impact on business and society.

In the age of creative destruction, human beings collaborating to find new creative solutions are critical to survival. To achieve this we need to remove old structures and norms where the old have the power, control and respect and instead create a reciprocal relationship between young and old.

We must let the young teach.

*

THIEF

INTRODUCTION

By Mark Earls, Founder of Herd Consulting

Sixty-second pitch: our ability to use the ideas and the brains of others – to steal, copy or borrow – is the most important super-power we have inherited from our human predecessors. It means we don't have to store information or know-how within our individual skulls but use the brains of others to do so – we *outsource the cognitive load*. Like all superpowers it can be used for good or ill, but not to use it at all – or not to acknowledge it – is to be dishonest to ourselves, our inheritance and our world. When used well, this is the way to create new ideas and things, faster, better and with more fun.

> *'The English, the English, the English are best.'*
> – Flanders and Swann

The English are a curious breed. Two millennia ago, the Roman Emperor Marcus Aurelius encouraged the readers of his stoical meditations on life and leadership to remember their special status in the universe as Roman citizens. At school, our history master confessed to reassuring himself with the fact that he would always be 'a Balliol man'. The English still have a very similar view of themselves. Whether it's the Old Etonian in a Notting Hill wine bar or the bedraggled England football fan who complains that 'other countries don't understand our drinking culture', there's something about being English that thrives on a sense of superiority over others.

It would be churlish to deny the English their pride in their many inventions and innovations – in science, engineering, art, literature and music and in the simple things like a cup of tea or the games they've taught the rest of us and let us beat them at them. The English enjoy a natural sense of superiority over the rest of us (even when penalties come round again), despite or perhaps because of the nation's refusal to learn to speak any other nation's language to any great extent.

Which always makes me, a Welshman born and bred, smile because from where I sit the greatest achievement of the English is their language. For a mongrel mix of north European, Scandinavian and Latin tribal tongues, English has become a truly global language. There are more than 335 million native speakers and many more that number who have a passing acquaintance with it. It spreads like wildfire, making pidgin and Creole versions of itself wherever it goes. English is continually sneaking into other cultures and languages (despite the best efforts of our friends in the Académie Française, who fight a sterling battle to keep anglophones out of France – a pc is an *ordinateur*. Really?).

And English only gets more popular. What do you say when someone wants you to smile into a camera? Each nation used to have their own word or phrase to crack facial features into a smile-like shape. In France, photographers used to call out marmoset (*ouistiti*); in Bulgaria, cabbage (*zele*); in Denmark, orange (*appelsin*); in much of Latin America, whisky (yesiree). More and more, unfortunately, the English language options for 'cheese' or the prosaic English injunction, 'smile', are catching on.

Which gives us a clue as to how English got to be so popular – it is relatively easy to speak a few words of English, to make a 'pidgin' version, such as those that have emerged in the far corners of the world to where the English and their fellow anglophones have traipsed. English is eminently copyable. Even Yoda a form of the mother tongue speaking does.

But English is a thief's tongue in another sense: it readily embraces the structures and forms of other languages. For example, the continuous tense ('I'm doing this . . .') is a relic of Celtic languages, unknown in other modern north European tongues. Other aspects of its grammar and syntax have roots in German, Norse and other north European languages that our Dark Age visitors brought with them. Significantly, it also bears the marks of other more recent invaders like the French (well, the Norman Conquest wasn't that recent, but you get the point). Many of our fancy words – like the words employed in the law, politics, eating and cooking – tend to be French in origin.

English continues to borrow from other languages. More than any of its European equivalents, the English dictionary contains so many foreign words, most of which native speakers imagine are English: cookie from the modern Dutch; ketchup from Cantonese and tea from Hokkien Chinese; avatar from Sanskrit; alcohol, alcove and admiral from Arabic; (good old) Blighty and bungalow from Hindi and Urdu; dollar and robot from Czech; cargo and canoe from Spanish; camouflage and casserole from the French; and, of course, flannel, lech and dad are all from the Welsh.

The success of the English language, then, is mostly down to copying and copyability. It's not a language that requires a linguistic police force to keep it pure (like the Académie Française); of course, there are sticklers for spelling and grammar obsessives (as with all languages) but, for the majority of speakers, the point about English is that it flexes and borrows.

COPY COPY COPY

We tend not to think of copying other people's ideas as a good thing, let alone a 'superpower'. In modern creative culture it's widely seen to be unfair, unnecessary and maybe even unethical to use (or be seen to be using) other people's ideas. (This brings to mind an old friend who once defined 'guilt' as 'that feeling you're supposed to have when someone catches you doing something they don't approve of').

To a self-identifying *Creative* (with a capital 'C') person, admitting to using other people's work or ideas is a critical sign of weakness; it undermines the reputation of the self-styled innovator. Sometimes we can get away with it by talking about our 'inspiration' or about the (heartfelt) tribute (*homage*, another fancy French word) our work pays to what inspired it. But few of us feel comfortable admitting to it: we praise originality and novelty, not familiarity and the previously loved/second-hand.

But copying is a superpower. If the explosion of behavioural cognitive science in the last decade has taught us one thing it's that copying – or 'social learning', to use the polite academic euphemism – is one of humanity's greatest gifts as a species. We are 'homo *mimicus*' as some put it, the *copying* rather than the wise or thinking ('sapiens') ape. It starts almost from the moment we're born (American psychologist Andrew Meltzow observed human infants copying as early as forty-two minutes post-partum) and we spend the rest of our lives harnessing the ability to outsource our thinking to those around us. It shapes the names we give our children, the clothes we wear, where we live, the music we listen to and where we go on vacation. It affects the products we buy and the attitudes we have to them and to each other. Even our ideas about what makes someone attractive or what a fair share looks like are borrowed from other people – they are not, as you might have assumed, 'fixed' in our biological selves.

The thing is, it is just such an efficient use of human minds; without copying each of us would need much more data storage capacity – we'd have to carry around so much more information in our individual heads. And, we'd have to think much harder, working from first principles every time a new challenge emerges (like getting dressed or deciding what's good and what's bad to eat). You'd have to do the math. Each and every time. Why bother, when you can outsource the load?

*

Being human means you never need to be on your own: you stand surrounded by all of humanity and have access to many more people's experience and know-how than you will ever meet. Some of this is encoded in what we call 'culture' – the shared assumptions and short cuts that we use to navigate a social world together with the people we meet; some of it is accessible through the connective technology of the age, in social media and the internet as a whole.

The point is this: none of us starts alone; none of us has to create alone.

GREAT MINDS

This is what all the great innovators and creative minds acknowledge (whatever else they tell their fans): Picasso famously observed that while talent copies, genius steals (Faris and Rosie Yakob, whose essay is the final one in this section, clearly agree – they named their company to underline the importance of this). T. S. Eliot insisted that the quality of a poet isn't determined by if but how they copy (and what they do with the source of copying). James Watt, the man my schoolbooks called the 'Father of the Industrial Revolution', didn't invent the steam engine; he improved Newcomen's fifty-year-old design by adding an external condenser. James Dyson didn't invent the vacuum cleaner, he merely enhanced it. Steve Jobs and his team at Apple Corp didn't 'invent' the desktop, the laptop, the tablet, the mobile phone or mobile music players. They took other people's ideas and did them better (or at least more simply).

*

David Bowie, probably the most influential figure in popular music for the last three decades, freely admitted to stealing from others – his breakthrough *Ziggy Stardust* was based on his reading of William Burroughs' *The Wild Boys*, *Diamond Dogs* on Orwell's *1984*, his *Berlin Trilogy* on the disturbing throb of Krautrock that he discovered while he was hiding out in Berlin with Iggy Pop. Even his creative techniques were borrowed from others – cut-up lyrics from Burroughs and co., calculated dislocation from Brian Eno and so on: 'The only art I'm interested in is art I can steal.'

FOR GOOD OR OTHERWISE . . .

Of course, you can use this superpower for good. Or for ill. Up to you.

You can make new and interesting things, things that solve problems, by using the stuff that (as artist Grayson Perry observes) is just lying around.

Or you can steal other people's ideas and re-present them as your own (that's what copyright law is supposed to hinder).

The choice is yours.

Unsurprisingly, 'bad faith' copying often happens when money comes into play. That's why the music industry is awash with copyright lawyers, why start-up pitches are full of spurious claims to exclusive IP and why businesses like Apple guard their IP so tightly (even why Chinese 'Shanzhai' copycat manufacturers are such a headache).

Sometimes status makes the thievery seem OK (and much worse when discovered). Hence the brouhaha about the third Mrs Trump's recycling of a recent speech by her predecessor as First Lady, the press kerfuffle thirty years ago about then would-be president Joe Biden borrowing heavily from a notable speech by UK Labour Party leader, Neil Kinnock, or Senator Lloyd Bentsen's challenge to VP candidate Dan Quayle in 1988: 'Senator, you're no Jack Kennedy.'

Sometimes, of course, the theft is clear but unintentional (or at least, unconscious). George Harrison ended up paying a fortune to the publishers of Johnny Mack's 'He's So Fine' because his strum-along hippy tune 'My Sweet Lord' was judged to be an unconscious copy of the song, made famous by The Chiffons.

LEARN TO CODE OR LEARN TO COPY

There's a popular mantra in many businesses today that the central skill of the twenty-first century must be the ability to code. I myself have learned a lot from doing the basics.

However, for my money, it's *far more important to learn how to copy and steal well* (as it happens, in learning the basics of coding you quickly discover that it's better to use other people's well-tested code than write everything yourself from scratch).

*

Copying – borrowing – thieving – whatever you call it – is the superpower you've got to get to grips with now. The sooner you do, the better and faster you'll be able to solve the problems in front of you, the better and the more voluminous the ideas you'll create and the more fun you'll have. Better Fresher Faster and More Fun (as Laura Jordan Bambach and I described in our keynote at Cannes Innovation Lions 2016).

What follows are three pieces that explore this superpower from different angles. First, prize-winning architect Alistair Barr reveals just how central thieving is to architects and the building world, how they've lied to themselves about it and how technology is making it easier to do good copying. Award-winning milliner Justin Smith talks openly and compellingly about the impossibility of not taking inspiration from around you and how happiness and creativity are interwoven. And, finally, Rosie and Faris Yakob of Genius Steals give us a very practical take on how to steal well in marketing and advertising.

Take what you can. I know I will.

COPY GOOD, COPY BAD, COPY SMARTER? ARE ARCHITECTS FINALLY LEARNING TO COPY INTELLIGENTLY AFTER 2,000 YEARS OF PRACTICE?

By Alistair Barr, Founder of Barr Gazetas

The young and artistic King Ludwig II wanted a perfect copy of Versailles on his island in eastern Bavaria in the late nineteenth century. By the completion of building works in 1885 he had spent nine centuries of accumulated family wealth on this project. His passion to create an exact copy of a famous piece of architecture led directly to this financial disaster and the demise of his kingdom. Ludwig was dethroned and later found dead, presumed murdered, in the lake at his 'Versailles'.

Architects are told this tragic story while training. Teachers use it as aversion therapy to warn student architects of the dangers of copying. The truth is that architects have always copied each other. It has been the case since Vitruvius published his *Ten Books on Architecture* in 20 BC.

By the twentieth century copying had been reduced to a guilty secret by superstar architects like Le Corbusier, who was erasing references and precedents from his published work in a ruthless bid to convince the world of his 'immaculate conceptions'. The profession has now spent a hundred years in denial, believing that originality is the holy grail of good architecture. Many of the post-war architectural horrors come from this brutal brainwashing at the schools of architecture. The cult of originality has created many carbuncles.

I strongly believe that this distrust of precedents has harmed the creative flow of architectural thought. However, things are changing. In the last ten years there has been an explosion of openness to current and proven examples available to copy. At last, we are processing ideas in an imaginative way.

GOOD, BAD AND DIFFERENT

In Roman Italy, Vitruvius wrote the first 'Books of Architecture'. In the Renaissance, Palladio and Alberti published guides to all architectural styles and building types. These guides were used to give examples for other architects to copy from as accepted practice and set classicism as the only appropriate style for public buildings. Vitruvius said, 'the frequent and continued contemplation of the mode of executing any given work will create architecture'. He was correct and tourists visiting Rome, Florence and Bath still marvel at the refined classicism. There was no shame in copying classical books and the 'orders' of architecture were expressed as the rulebooks of ideal ratios of dimensions and proportions.

Affluent noblemen went on the Grand Tours to see classical architecture in situ. Observation, sketching and careful measuring to copy and truly understand architectural principles was the norm. These tours were highly fashionable and gave you bragging rights for years to come.

The great Gothic cathedrals of northern Europe had also followed very strict design precedents. The master masons began as apprentices and learned Gothic detailing from generation to generation. The masons would move from site to site taking their accumulated knowledge with them. This social learning of the great cathedrals and palaces has created enduring masterpieces.

CAPITOL COPYING

When the State Capitol was completed in Washington, DC, in 1800 its neoclassical architecture became the template for almost every other state capital in the USA. The state governments used copying to achieve instant gravitas in their buildings. Architectural historian Charles Jencks notes that the neoclassical style became the signifier of safe, solid government.

By the nineteenth century, engineering and technology gave architects a chance to embrace new ways of building. However, this was still within recognised stylistic parameters. Once the architect had decided on a classical or Gothic style there were many examples available to follow. The Victorian 'Style Wars' reached a bizarre crisis at the Houses of Parliament when Charles Barry designed a classical, symmetrical layout that Augustus Pugin then decorated with Gothic details. 'All Grecian, Sir, Tudor details on a Classic body,' said Pugin.

*

In the 1920s, Le Corbusier was widely believed to be truly original. In reality, he followed many precedents, but his self-publicity emphasised originality as the only way forward. Generations of architects followed these principles of originality because he had carefully hidden all the clues of his creative theft and homages. Given Le Corbusier's strength of feeling about 'copying' it is ironic that so many architects did not possess the talent to be original and ended up copying him.

In the 1950s architects began to visit France to worship at the 'shrine of Le Corbusier'. Post-war currency restriction and long-distance travel complications meant that middle-class men (they were nearly always men) visited Marseilles' Unité d'habitation and a few other Le Corbusier buildings obsessively.

As a consequence, there are many (mostly inferior) copies. The Alton Estate in Roehampton is a sobering example. In their excitement the architects had forgotten the climatic differences between Mediterranean Marseilles and damp south-west London, with disastrous consequences. Much of sixties and seventies designs suffer from blind copying of a very small pool of examples and we are living with the aesthetic and social consequences of this restrictive copying.

THE TURNING POINT: MORE, MORE, MORE

At last, however, there is an end to 2,000 years of using restricted precedents. Easy travel and the number of web images have widened the architecture gene pool in the last fifteen years. At last it is OK to copy creatively.

'Stair Porn' was one of the first websites to show an incredible mix of styles, ideas and precedents for stairs for everyone to copy unashamedly. This site has inspired a wave of other sites giving aspiring architects access to every possible precedent. Yet early adopter architects still kept their 'homages' secret. The stair site name plays on the architect's guilt at copying.

I believe unprecedented access to innovative architectural styles should be celebrated. If the examples to be copied are examined in a rigorous manner they will stimulate a richness of architectural talent that has not been seen for over a hundred years.

I have been a part-time tutor at the University of Greenwich School of Architecture for over twenty-five years. The changes in precedent references have been massive and the quality of design is getting better as a result.

Tutorial sessions used to move very slowly with few creative leaps. Similar projects would be referenced but visual references would be slow to find. The key library book would be lost and the magazine references would be badly printed with useless descriptions. One well-thumbed magazine would end up as the only reference with resulting banality of design aspirations.

These days a tutorial will have a laptop as an essential member. A rapid-fire conversation will occur while we access a wide range of examples. These images act as a catalyst for design conversations that can freely range across every possible precedent.

A good building is a complex object which needs to function on many levels. An open mind and a varied selection of ideas is needed. The technical execution of a project is crucial. This 'technical tutoring' used to be a turgid discussion around a few textbooks and out-of-date catalogues. The technology now enhances the design because we can see what has been achieved before. We call this 'intelligent referencing'.

There is an obvious drawback to this design process that I am describing as a weak student may just create crude copies.

However, this 'intelligent referencing' can help the weaker students understand the complexities of high-level design. The process encourages synthesis of ideas and, with a diverse range of ideas to digest, students begin to realise how rich the process of architectural design can be.

PIRATE ARCHITECTS

There can be drawbacks to this new openness to embrace precedents and it is not just weak students who copy crudely. When architects copy in a creative and critical manner great projects can be achieved. However, weak or lazy architects may be tempted simply to make a carbon copy without a second thought. These architects have been called out by the late Zaha Hadid. In Beijing, Hadid designed the Wangjing Soho building as a composition of two pebble-shaped buildings. She then had to take legal action against 'pirate architects' in Chongqing in 2013 who simply reproduced her design. Hadid argued that if a copy showed innovative mutations she would be excited and that 'it is fine to take from the same well, but not from the same bucket'. Copying can create new forms but only if there is an understanding of the reasons behind the original idea. The developers of the Chongqing towers have claimed they 'never meant to copy, only to surpass' which may be the future catch-all excuse for designers.

THROWING IT ALL AWAY

Five years ago my practice, Barr Gazetas, threw away our entire paper technical library. A court had ruled that if an architect only referred to technical details on paper there was too much out-of-date material. If a component failed, the architect would be legally liable for not being up to date. With our paper library gone, we only reference completely up-to-date technical specifications online. This gives us confidence that we are using the correct knowledge in our research.

Our office uses all the precedents available to grow our design aspirations. There are examples across the world that show clients what can be achieved and how it would look. Our mood boards show any reference, however obscure, and we use this to actively raise clients' expectations. Good architects have always collaged together ideas to create new expressions.

*

A recent example of this is our fit-out for Anomaly, a global creative agency with offices in Shanghai, Amsterdam, New York and Los Angeles. For their London office design we analysed all the disparate architectural elements in the other offices. When we understood the essence of them we copied the forms but with a critical attitude. Great architects can now use their copying super-power to study and learn from every possible type of building expression.

This accessibility is making architects more aware and more open to new ideas. Our problem-solving skills can lead to great designs, but innovation only comes when there are enough examples to act as a true catalyst. Architects have been copying each other for 2,000 years, sometimes explicitly, more often in a furtive and slightly guilty way. In recent years the access to precedents has been such that it has significantly expanded the well of inspiration. This makes it an exciting time to be an architect. We have finally shaken off old restrictions and are free to explore and create great architecture and design, using stimulus from anywhere and everywhere.

HATS AND HAPPINESS

Mark Earls interviews Justin Smith Esq,
Founder of J Smith Esquire

On an unnaturally warm May evening, a gaggle of happy men and women, young and old, tumble out from a well-known Mayfair fine art gallery, all smiles and giggles and clouds of cigarette smoke and vape plumes. As if this is their first taste of summer after a long, dark winter, they sniff the surprisingly gentle air, laughing and smoking and joking and preening and laughing some more.

Look more closely and you'll notice that many are distinctively dressed – some are wrapped in bohemian formals; others have a shock of this summer's colour in their hair or around their shoulders. Some have distinctive and artful tattoos and piercings; some have paint on their trousers or in their hair that gives them away. And a number of them – many more than you normally expect to see in twenty-first-century London – are wearing hats. Unusual hats, familiar shapes in unusual material or size; hats that say 'wear me now'.

Inside the gallery, on mannequins and busts, in bell jars and in glass cases, is some of the most beautiful and smile-inducing headwear you will ever be lucky enough to wear. Hats that are like feline masks, with incredible hand-sewn gold detailing, sensible trilbies made from leopard-skin print, a wonderful golden leather hat-wig, a turban in python skin, a simple flat cap made from gold-painted leather and beautiful opera hats in soft, faded velvet.

Tonight is the preview party for the latest collection of J Smith Esq, an award-winning milliner and teacher. A nicer, gentler soul you'll never meet – not at all what you'd expect from the man whose work is bought by celebrities like Angelina Jolie and Amal Clooney, designers like Stella McCartney and sharp-eyed filmmakers (he was responsible for the magnificent headdress Jolie wore in the 2014 film *Maleficent* and the stylish noir hats of the 2015 remake of *The Man from U.N.C.L.E.*).

DOWN SOUTH

A week later, I'm in Justin's south London studio, old stables now lovingly furnished by vintage wooden lockers from a boys' school, old leather suitcases, windows dangling with plants, daybeds, antique mirrors and an enormous and well-stocked tropical aquarium. It's also home to his vintage hat lasts and presses and the collection that he made with them. I'm here to talk about his approach to work, about creativity and copying, about influence and inspiration.

It's amazing to see your hats in the gallery, curated to show the artistry involved in your work, rather than on a shelf or in a shop. How did you feel seeing them?

I loved it – it's nice to see them treated as 3D objects . . . my work is quite sculptural and hats do this well. Unlike a pair of trousers, a hat doesn't need to have a pocket here or there or a crotch to make it wearable. Hats don't have any of those limitations. You can just explore . . .

So you don't just design them?

No, some people work that way – have an idea, make a sketch and send it off. I make the hats, too. All of them are sewn by hand by me [laughs], well, most of them. Some of them are very catwalk but many of them aren't. As I get older, I'm finding myself making hats that I want to wear myself, which I didn't do before – the perfect flat cap – but, yes, the gallery is a great place to look at all of these different hats as pieces rather than just things to stick on a head.

When you look at the collection displayed this way, is the thing that inspired each piece still clear to you?

Sometimes, yes – the python-skin turban I first did about five years ago. A designer got me the material for a show because I'd said I always wanted to work with it. I didn't think much about it at the time so just threw it together and sent it down the runway. I knew I could do it better so when I was doing this show, I took it apart and remade it and I think it works much better now.

But much of the time, I couldn't tell you what inspired me, because I start with a feeling and some material and a little thought I've got somewhere in the back of my mind. When you start to work with the material, your idea changes and something new emerges. Sometimes it feels a bit like magic but quite often you don't know where you started from or worry about where it's going. I've always been OK with that.

The process of making things is really important to you then?

Yes, I'm a maker. Always have been. I've cooked and cut hair, made shoes and clothes before. When I'm not doing this, I'll be making a shed (a sunny shed built mostly from recycled windows sits in the yard outside the studio) or I'll go up to the allotment and build a picket fence. I've always been happier making.

So where does your inspiration come from?

[Laughs] . . . everyone wants to know that. Inspiration isn't the problem – I'm always getting inspiration. It's everywhere. All of the time. If something resonates with me it'll stick and come out later. Filtering it can be an issue as I can get too much [going on inside] . . . If I see something I like I might file a picture or sample away in an actual folder or I might do the same thing unconsciously in my memory. Then, sometime later, it pops out while I'm working on a piece.

Some people do active research – actively chasing inputs – it doesn't sound like that's you, or does it?

No, I love going to [places like] the V&A to see beautiful things and wonder how they're made, but it'll often be something small, a small detail that sticks with me. The colour of a piece of stained glass, for example. Or the feel of a piece of material.

You have certain hat styles you come back to again and again, like the flat cap which appears in this collection in gold leather and in Chinese painted silk finish. You also recycle pieces from previous collections – reworked and remade. Are you OK with copying yourself and working within traditions?

[Laughs] I'm always trying to do things better. I used to just want to know how to do something, get it done and move on. I've learned that as I rework things I learn more and I learn I've learned new things, too. Some shapes work really well and are popular, but, because each piece is hand-made and because I'm concentrated on the materials, each one really is different. Even two parts of the same sheet of gold leather will behave and work differently in two different hats. It's always different.

The fashion world is well-known for its hype and histrionics. How do you cope? You've always seemed pretty sane and normal to me.

[Laughs] I've learned to, I think. I've always liked clothes and style but never really liked the behaviour that the fashion world encourages. It's not really me. Parties and so on, and people you're supposed to be impressed by. The pieces I make are often striking and surprising; they work for people who want to stand out, but that's not really the point for me. It's a by-product of the thing I'm excited about – the process of making.

Is work when you're happiest, then?

Yes, I suppose so. I'm always making. I really like teaching, too.

You're very generous with your skills and knowledge.

Well, I don't know about that, but nobody teaches these skills and techniques now. I was quite determined to learn them when I started. I recently started teaching again at Pinewood Studios with people who'd been working in film and costume for a number of years but making hats as a hobby. They'll bring in [for example] a historical re-enactment hat that they have been working on. I didn't know what re-enactment was to be honest [laughs]. They ask me how to make that particular hat. I often don't know the answer but it's always much better to get them to think it through for themselves. How do you think people made this hat? What does the material and the stitching tell you? And we'd work it out together. I learn something new and they develop their own style and ability to work with materials. I could do it for them – could bully them into doing what I would do – but what's the point? I wouldn't enjoy making them copy my style and the finished product would be all the same.

When I think about my work and how it's rooted in the knowledge and experience of people who've gone before, I find it very inspiring to be part of a chain.

Yes, the ideas and the skills need to be kept alive and passed on. Nobody seems to be teaching them today. It's good to keep the skills going. It feels good.

You love being in the process and in particular you seem really comfortable with not knowing how things are going to turn out. I think this is one of the most important things for a creative person of any sort. It makes me think of a Canadian improv theatre group I once came across who used to say 'Trust the Moose. The Moose will provide.'

[Laughs] Yes, but it's weird, isn't it? But you just get caught up in the making of things and then . . . somehow . . . every time it kind of works.

How does that play out when somebody does the making for you?

It's different. When I've worked that way before – designing and making a prototype, sending it off to the factory – it's disappointing when everything comes back and it's not what you intended. It's copied – they've followed the design – but it's not the same thing at all. It's like the spirit is missing . . . the spirit of the material. So I've learned to do things differently: to ask them how *they* think we could make the pieces be brilliant, how *they* could get the best out of the materials. To do it *their* way. More of a collaboration.

And when you're working to someone else's brief?

When I work in films, it's best when it's with a designer or director who has a clear idea that I can do something with. So, for example, with *The Man from U.N.C.L.E.*, I've always really loved old black and white movies so I knew where to go. But it's better if they have the confidence and trust to let me go off and explore and do my own thing. To let me come back with a great answer given the way I work. When people are vague and double-guessing each other it works less well. It's the relationship between us that makes it.

AFTER THE SHOW

Justin Smith is one of most creative people you'll meet, but disarmingly so. It's genuinely refreshing to see and feel the world the way he does. Inspiration – the raw material of his creativity – is everywhere. His world is full of wonder and delight. Like other creative people, he seems to view the world as a treasure trove of starting points, of tentative first thoughts and maybe-maybes. He's happy to borrow – from himself, from collaborators and anywhere that resonates inside himself – to make something new and fresh each and every time. He also seems to give as much back as he takes: teaching and passing on the skills. It's not like this is some professional stance – his 'creative identity' – it's his natural way of being. It's his superpower.

SAME SAME BUT DIFFERENT: HOW ABSTRACTION IS THE KEY TO CREATIVITY

By Faris Yakob with Rosie Yakob, founders of Genius Steals

ABSTRACT: In order to further develop the Genius Steals theory of creativity, the authors establish a foundation of abstraction, dismantle the notion of originality and develop a schema for understanding 'stealing' and recombination in the formation of ideas.

THESIS

1. Same Same But Different.
2. Abstraction.
3. Metaphor.

SYNTHESIS

1. Originality Is a Myth.
2. Ideas Are New Combinations.

PRAXIS

1. Transposition.
2. The Spectrum of Stealing.
3. Articulation.

THESIS

1. SAME SAME BUT DIFFERENT

One of the great things about travelling is learning new things, or new ways to look at things you already knew. Travellers to Thailand rapidly encounter an expression used ubiquitously by natives, one which, on the face of it, is a paradox. How can something be 'same same but different?' The Thai people use this phrase in innumerable situations. Western tourists (*farang* in Thai) often encounter it transactionally, where substitute goods (and occasionally gender) are offered up for purchase instead of the specific item you might have requested.

The expression flowed out into the world on backpacker trails and bounced back onto t-shirts in Thailand, as culture is so often captured, codified and commoditised. Its origin is mysterious but it appears to be a direct translation of a native phrase – doubling up words for emphasis is common in Thai – *khlai khlai tae mai meuan*, which means 'similar but not the same'. As is often the case, this literal translation of a native construct spits out something that isn't quite what was intended. Once in a while, however, that process of translation is transformative and articulates a much more interesting idea.

How can something be 'same same but different?' Let's start with abstraction.

2. ABSTRACTION

Abstraction is, arguably, the most important human cognitive skill and the source of much, if not all, human creativity. Very simply, it is the process by which we derive general rules and concepts from specific examples. In this section, we steal from David Foster Wallace's meditation on abstraction in his book on the nature of infinity, *Everything and More*.

The word abstraction is derived from the adjectival *abstractus*, 'drawn away'. The dictionary provides numerous definitions, of which the most important for our line of thinking is 'withdrawn or separated from matter, from practice, or from particular example'. Also relevant is the meaning of reducing something to its essence, as in the above abstract of this essay.

> *'Abstraction has all kinds of problems and headaches built in, we all know. Part of the hazard is how we use nouns. We think of noun's meanings in terms of denotations. Nouns stand for things – man, desk, pen, David, head, aspirin. A special kind of comedy results when there's confusion about what's a real noun, as in "Who's on first?" or those Alice in Wonderland routines – "What can you see on the road?" "Nothing." "What great eyesight! What does nothing look like?"'*
>
> – David Foster Wallace

Faris likes to tell an anti-joke about this. 'I want to do a stand-up show where I come on stage and just say "Language is ambiguous" and then walk off', he's been known to say. This is because, at a certain level of abstraction, many (if not most) jokes rely on this single fact. And, of course, by definition, the same is true for all puns, which leads to many punning advertising taglines, and practically all British tabloid headlines.

Part of abstraction is reduction and part is classification, which allows for various levels of abstraction:

> 'Let's say "man" meaning some particular man is Level One.
> "Man" meaning the species is Level Two. Something like
> "humanity" or "humanness" is Level Three; now we're talking
> about the abstract criteria for something qualifying as human.
> And so forth.'
> — David Foster Wallace

Abstraction is both how we learn and how we then apply what we have learned. It allows us to distil patterns from specifics, concepts from experiences, and then see applications that may not have been visible on the surface.

3. METAPHOR

What's a metaphor?
I don't know, what is it for?

Metaphors, as every schoolchild is taught, are not similes. They are not simply descriptions that use a direct comparison of two things across a quality: *as white as snow* being a canonical example of a simile.

Rather, metaphors operate at a higher level of abstraction, referring to one thing by mentioning another thing to which it's not *literally* related. Metaphors are ubiquitous in human speech, exposing the ways in which we think. Simple metaphors about space are particularly common (as cognitive linguists like Stephen Pinker have explored at length) probably because we evolved to understand how to deal with and thus talk about spatial relationships first. [Where is the water? It's over there, on the right, behind that rock.] When we say, 'I'm feeling down' to mean depressed, we are using a spatial metaphor.

Higher order metaphors are more complex and considered. Aristotle was particularly interested in those kinds of metaphors. He wrote that 'the greatest thing by far is to have a command of metaphor; . . . it is the mark of genius, for to make good metaphors implies an eye for resemblances.' 'As pure as snow' is a metaphor used by Shakespeare in reference to Macbeth in his play of the same name.

Resemblances being, of course, same same but different. Inherent in the idea of a metaphor is an understanding of levels of abstraction.

Aristotle described the process of expressing the relationship between the two elements of a metaphor (which are called the *tenor* and the *vehicle*, the terms themselves being metaphors, of course) as one of transference:

'Metaphor is the application of an alien name by transference either from genus to species, or from species to species, or by analogy, that is proportion.' (He's describing what we would understand as metaphor and metonymy.)

The metaphors we use both reflect and change the way we think. The 'war on (drugs, poverty, homelessness)' metaphor used heavily in American political rhetoric reflects the military mindset of the government and impacts how policy is then made. The implications within the metaphor have driven policy to be bellicose, which has been incredibly and necessarily destructive, since that quality is inherent in the metaphor.

Effective metaphors, according to Aristotle, are 'lucid, pleasing and strange', which suggests both clarity in meaning and luminosity, fun or satisfying to hear, and un-obvious.

SYNTHESIS

1. ORIGINALITY IS A MYTH

'Nothing is original. Steal from anywhere that resonates with inspiration or fuels your imagination.

'Devour old films, new films, music, books, paintings, photographs, poems, dreams, random conversations, architecture, bridges, street signs, trees, clouds, bodies of water, light and shadows. Select only things to steal from that speak directly to your soul. If you do this, your work (and theft) will be authentic.

'Authenticity is invaluable; originality is non-existent. And don't bother concealing your thievery – celebrate it if you feel like it. In any case, always remember what Jean-Luc Godard said: "It's not where you take things from – it's where you take them to."'

— Jim Jarmusch

This quote was reimagined as an image which then spread around the internet in early 2009. It's still finding its way to us in this form today.

But the desire for originality is still pervasive, so let's tackle this notion head-on.

Modern conceptions of originality don't really make any sense. They are vaguely religious, as though creativity were prophetic work, accessing the unknowable through mystical means. Innovation, or creativity, is often romantically depicted as making something out of nothing.

'The act of creation is about making something happen, from nothing. That's creativity,' said Dave Trott, the brilliant, legendary advertising creative director and prolific writer on creativity.

Since language is ambiguous so is, of course, Mr Trott's meaning. (Remember the quote from *Alice in Wonderland*: 'What does *nothing* look like?')

In the sense of creating something where there was previously not something, this is both true and obvious. In the sense of creating something *out of nothing*, it is impossible, unless we are to under-stand human creativity as being akin to the prime mover of the universe (however you may conceive of that), instead of as being a product of culture.

Trott's quote continues: 'Just making things nicer isn't creativity. That's styling', which I'm sure stylists may take umbrage at – but it suggests he means it in the first sense.

Here's a good example of this notion, this ambiguity, confusing people. It comes from an interview with the incredibly smart and influential advertising thinker Adam Morgan from *Milk Magazine*.

Adam wrote *Eating the Big Fish* and it has been said that he 'invented' the notion of challenger brands: brands that operate at a counterpoint to the prevailing trends in their category (although he points out that the book didn't invent anything, it just made some techniques of creative thinkers 'visible to everyone in the same way at the same time').

In the interview he describes some of the changes in his thinking since it was written, and one area he is looking to explore is 'opportunity'.

'Do you know who invented the cheeseburger?' asks Morgan. 'It was JWT in the 1930s, on behalf of Kraft slices who wanted to encourage the American population to increase their consumption of cheese slices. JWT suggested that they attach them as an ingredient to the most popular meal in America – the hamburger. They created something out of nothing.'

I love this story – the idea that an advertising agency helped create a new usage occasion, a new reason to buy a product, and forever changed American culture just by taking two existing things and putting them together. (An inherently combinatorial idea if ever I ate one.)

Another reason I love this story is that it's almost certainly *not true*.

Wikipedia says that the cheeseburger was invented in 1924 by a sixteen-year-old fry cook called Lionel Sternberger at a sandwich shop in Pasadena, California. (What are the odds his name would have 'burger' in it? Is that nominal determinism at work?)

I very much doubt that this was the first time anyone added cheese to a burger, but it's the first recorded instance (according to Virginia Woolf, nothing is real until it has been recorded) and it certainly predates the 1930s.

Assuming the Kraft/JWT story is at all true – I can find no further evidence online, but that's not conclusive either way – what's way more likely is that some inspiring young Mad Man saw, heard of or indeed ate a cheeseburger, stole the idea, and then, perhaps, the agency and the brand helped spread it from California, which has long been the progenitor of 'new' ideas in America (yoga from India, sushi from Japan), across the country. Further, Kraft cheese slices themselves were invented to find a way to deal with the vast amount of milk that the American government had caused to be produced through aggressive subsidies for dairy farmers. And so forth.

Stories are often more compelling than facts, and origin stories have a particular resonance, but no idea comes from nowhere. Sternberger didn't create the cheeseburger from nothing, he invented it from cheese slices and burgers, both of which very much existed prior to his new combination.

This pure idea of originality doesn't make sense. Originality as conceived, 'born fully formed' from the head of Zeus as Athena was, is incoherent. It expresses the sensation, not the actuality, of imagination – if any idea had no relation to existing ideas, would we even understand it?

How far back do you go to claim originality? No previously used media? No previously deployed concepts? No previously used words? Since that would obviously render culture impossible to create, creativity obviously must be iterative, building upon itself.

The cartoonist and animator Nina Paley puts it beautifully: 'Nothing is original. For a work to have meaning, it must use language – it must "make sense." It needs to work with memes already living in the host mind: language, images, melodies, patterns. It can't be wholly original. It can hardly be original at all.' To briefly revisit the metaphorical description of character 'as pure as snow', we're reminded that this requires a cultural understanding of both snow, and the idea that white represents purity, which is only the case in some cultures.

Originality is a decidedly modern fetish. It only became highly regarded as a creative value around the time of the Romantic poets, who largely characterised our notion of originality. Shakespeare famously 'evinced a marked propensity for avoiding unnecessary invention', according to the copyright academic Alexander Lindey.

The Romantic poets' obsession with originality was likely a consequence of various cultural forces of their time, especially the beginning of mass industrialisation and the recession of God from intellectual discourse. This led to the consequent question of creativity being an inherently feminine quality, since only women create life, which the predominantly male poets didn't particularly like the idea of.

These concerns aside, because our current context is at least somewhat different, we can comfortably assert that 'nothing will come of nothing', to quote Shakespeare, who was quoting Lucretius, who was paraphrasing Parmenides. And so forth.

See what we mean?

2. IDEAS ARE NEW COMBINATIONS

With the first sections covered, we have almost all the components we need – but we lack a way to put them together.

*

Here we steal from advertising luminary James Webb Young, who wrote one of the shortest and most useful treatises on creativity, called *Ideas Are New Combinations*.

If originality is a myth, then why isn't everything exactly the same? From whence do we get novelty, or the (re)semblance thereof? As Mark Earls points out in his book *Copy, Copy, Copy*, copying with errors provides one mechanism, allowing for things to drift from their original form into something different, and sometimes those differences create a new idea (same, same, but different).

However, the key mechanism for creating new from existing is the driver of all innovation in natural world: recombination.

Sexual reproduction involves taking randomised elements from two genomes and splicing them together. It produces endless novelty from the same source material – you do not look exactly like any of your siblings and never will, unless you are made from the same exact code, as twins are (and even then there can be epigenetic drift, which means you will have different phenotypes because of different contexts, but this technicality is less relevant for what we're talking about).

No matter where you look, there is no requirement for the kind of originality that comes from nothing.

Ideas at a conceptual level operate much the same way. This is why brainstorming exercises involve finding ways to mix things together: random words from a dictionary or relevant pieces of inspiration, applied to a problem or topic at hand. As Aristotle noted, to find a way to combine elements requires an ability to see resemblances or relationships between them, which is more abstract the less related the two things are.

Good ideas are non-obvious, non-trivial combinations that work, intellectually and for the job at hand. The most satisfying are the ones that take on the qualities of effective metaphors: They are 'lucid, pleasing and strange'. Something obvious is not creative. The least obvious combination that solves the problem at hand is the most effective, *because* it is less obvious, more interesting and less likely to have been explored before, ad nauseum.

Indeed, the dynamic tension between the diversity of the elements that still hold together is often what we mean when we say something is creative.

PRAXIS

1. TRANSPOSITION

'A good poet will usually borrow from authors remote in time, or alien in language, or diverse in interest.' – T. S. Eliot

Fishing endlessly from the same pool will rapidly demonstrate diminishing returns. Inbreeding makes for ever weaker genetic stock, more susceptible to genetic problems and diseases. Contrarily, outbreeding from diverse sources creates what is known as hybrid vigour, the tendency to show qualities superior to those of both parents.

In this quote Eliot is talking about poetry. It comes from the urtext that spawned the 'fauxtation' (a fake quotation, as so many are, assigned to famous people but with no textual reference) we named our company after – 'talent imitates, genius steals' – but it applies equally to all ideas.

Stealing from as diverse a pool as possible leads to better ideas. A creative mind is driven by curiosity to explore many domains of knowledge, and instinctively finds the similar patterns, the resemblances across them. Without any source materials, we cannot have ideas. This is why the words for memory and creativity are linked: one cannot invent without inventory.

Once a pattern has been recognised, it can be transposed into a different domain, to see if it's fertile there. This is how George de Mestral lifted the cocklebur from nature and invented Velcro. This is why breakthroughs in science, particularly where experts have been stuck for a long time, are often solved by scientists of *adjacent* specialisms – they know enough of the relevant topic but have new patterns to try to apply.

The danger of becoming too deeply expert in one singular thing, as we are so often driven to in a modern culture that encourages specialisation rather than generalisation, is that one might become what the Germans call a *Fachidiot*.

*

Fachidiot, which translated literally into English means 'subject idiot', is defined as: 'Someone who knows a lot about a particular field, in a similar way to a one-track specialist. The difference is that a one-track specialist still notices what is going on around him. A *Fachidiot* simply doesn't . . .'

2. THE SPECTRUM OF STEALING

At this point, hopefully we all agree: nothing is original. But even still, there is a clear ontological difference between inspiration, imitation, quoting and plagiarism and, to a great degree, they depend on both the level of abstraction and the intention:

- **Plagiarism** is passing off another's words as your own.
- **Quotation** outs itself as being someone else's words, which one may use 'in order the better to express' oneself, to quote Michel de Montaigne.
- **Imitation** is how we learn, copying craft.
- **Inspiration** takes the idea up one level of abstraction.

It's the difference between a forged Picasso painting, a Picasso image printed into a bricolage, a copied Picasso painting by a student and someone painting in the Cubist style.

There is a threshold for originality, as we understand it, a threshold beneath which people accept passive recombination – being influenced by the culture around you, which is why, say, art from the same period all tends to look alike, why there are movements – and active recombination: using pre-existing culture as part of the palette.

*

The idea of originality as having some specific threshold is enshrined in law, but where that threshold lies is unclear. Quotation is protected, sampling music is not. Although a sample was cleared for usage, the band The Verve was successfully sued over their hit 'Bittersweet Symphony' by the band they sampled, The Rolling Stones. Because a court decided they had used 'too much' of the sample, Keith Richards and Mick Jagger became the legal 'authors' of the song. This kind of cultural rentier action is hard for a cut'n'paste generation to understand as anything but greed, as it locks ideas down, diminishing culture, rather than opening it up.

Sometimes this happens unintentionally. Mark Earls, whose study of humanity's herd-like behaviour led to his insights around copying as the primary mechanism of both learning and progress, points out in his intro to this section: 'George Harrison ended up paying a fortune to the publishers of Johnny Mack's 'He's So Fine' because his strumalong hippy tune, 'My Sweet Lord' was judged to be an unconscious copy of the song, made famous by The Chiffons.'

A similar thing happened to singer Sam Smith, who voluntarily agreed to give a co-writing credit of his Grammy award-winning hit 'Stay With Me' to Tom Petty once it was pointed out that his song was structurally almost identical to Petty's 'I Won't Back Down'. This happens all the time because the way our brains create is hidden from our conscious mind, so we have the sensation of having an idea which is really just a memory. This is called cryptomnesia. We believe that the taboo around copying makes it even more likely. Artists and creators tend to be more aware of how they use and adapt their influences. As Tom Petty said of the settlement: 'No hard feelings. These things happen. Most times you catch it before it gets out the studio door, but in this case it got by.'

However, it's important to remember that this kind of thinking only applies when stealing the form, rather than the concept, of an idea. Move up one level of abstraction and copyright is irrelevant.

3. ARTICULATION

> '*And as imagination bodies forth*
> *The forms of things unknown, the poet's pen*
> *Turns them to shapes and gives to airy nothing*
> *A local habitation and a name*'
>
> – A Midsummer Night's Dream

Creativity must be divided into two parts, as indeed it is inside creative companies. In stage one, concepts are generated. Once a concept is decided upon, it is developed into articulations, which is the domain of craft; of writing, design, painting, printing, filmmaking, editing, software, fabrication, and so forth.

Each is a different mode of articulation that requires different skills, honed over time. Every language is a cultural artefact that evolves through the same processes that drive all evolution, constantly changing as errors creep into the discourse and are either abandoned or embraced. Each language maps differently from the human experience, which is why there are always words that cannot be simply translated, because they aren't just noises but symbols linked to other symbols in a web of concepts. Same same but different, refracted through several different cultures, emerged as a sticky aphorism in English (or perhaps Globish as the global form is sometimes called), a tight unit of language that expresses a cultural tension, a paradox to be managed, not a riddle that can be solved.

Concepts, however, are the domain of all human minds. Creativity is not to be conflated with craft, lest we render the human race in its entirety to fall outside of the creative department and what glorious, absurd hubris that would be. Creativity is a function of abstraction, and it is uniquely and universally human.

So, let us finish by abstracting the Genius Steals creative process:

- How can we expose ourselves to the most diverse set of influences, looking for non-obvious relationships, abstracting principles and concepts?
- How might we combine and recombine the elements?
- Can we transpose the patterns to distant domains of knowledge?
- Is the result, once articulated, 'lucid, pleasing and strange'?
- How best to put it into the world, to make it public, to publish it and see what someone else can make from it?

We chose an essay in this book, and we can't wait to see what you do.

EXERCISES

INDIVIDUAL EXERCISES

BREAKING A PROBLEM DOWN (HACKING)

This exercise is to get you in the habit of breaking bigger problems down into smaller bits. As Gareth Kay, founding partner of Zeus Jones, said in our last book, 'Hacks, by definition, are more effective. They take big complicated problems that can be more easily solved, whatever the solution takes. As a result, they remove the gap between the commercial imperative and the creative solution.'

All you need is pen, paper and Post-it notes.

Step 1
Take a big problem (e.g. gender equality in the workplace).

Step 2
Break the problem down into smaller parts.

E.g. for gender equality in the workplace it might be:
- Unconscious bias.
- Gender pay gap.
- Parental leave.
- Men's resistance to change.

Step 3

Take each of these smaller parts and break them down one step further.

E.g. for parental leave it might be:
- Gap between maternity leave and paternity leave.
- Cost of childcare.
- Lack of flexible working hours.
- Reluctance for men to take shared parental leave (due to cultural issues).
- The gender pay gap.

Step 4

Keep on doing this until you can't get any further (some may stop sooner than others).

Step 5

For each end point, think of one thing you can do to solve that problem. How might you change your behaviour as a business or as an individual? Write these down as a list.

Step 6

Commit to make ten changes over a three-month period. Write them down and at the end of each month monitor your progress and the impact it has had on the problem.

Repeat process as required.

THE POMODORO TECHNIQUE (HACKING)

This technique can be effective at hacking your productivity. All you need is a Pomodoro timer (or you can simply use https:// tomato-timer.com/ or download one of the many apps available), some work to do and some discipline.

1. Choose a task you want to complete.
2. Set the Pomodoro to twenty-five minutes (the Pomodoro is the timer).
3. Work on the task (without distractions) until the time runs out.
4. Take a short break (five minutes).
5. Then repeat for a maximum of three times.
6. Once you've completed four cycles, take a long break or do something completely different.

Note: if you are distracted at all during the Pomodoro you need to stop the process and start all over again, so make sure that you are free from distractions (mobile phones off, ensure that you are in a quiet place where you won't be disturbed, etc.).

TWO APPROACHES (MAKER)

This exercise is specifically aimed at anyone working in the communications industry and challenges you simply to look at a problem from two different angles; feel free to try it whatever sector you work in. All you will need is pen and paper and time for thinking.

Imagine a human problem. It can be emotional, social or functional. For example, it can be about getting fit, or reading more books, being more efficient at work or improving one's diet.

Once you have imagined a problem (it can be one of the above, or another problem that's dear to your heart), think about what a 'traditional' brand solution would be. Would it be a message, an inspirational image, a social campaign or something else?

Now, put your maker hat on. If you were asked to build a solution from scratch, how would you go about it? Who would you invite to join your team? What would be your experience design, visual design, production and distribution consideration? How would you test that you have the right product–market fit? How would you get your product in the hands of consumers? Who would you select to test your product first?

*

Compare the two approaches. What are the benefits of each? Where (if at all) do each of them fall short? Can they be combined?

When you figure out the strengths and weaknesses of each approach, imagine a company that does both. How would it look like organisationally? How would it look talent-wise? Which departments would it have? How would it fit in the wider ecosystem? What would its advantages be?

POSTCARD TO YOURSELF (MAKER/TEACHER)

Twenty minutes

This exercise is a fun way to sum up what you've learned from this book and give you a physical reminder of some of the things it inspired you to do.

You will need:
- A blank postcard.
- A stamp.
- Post-it notes (or 'Artefact cards*').
- Coloured pens or pencils.

Step 1 (five minutes)
Write down as many things as possible that you took out of reading the book (each point should be written on a separate Post-it note or Artefact card).

Step 2 (six minutes)
Close your eyes. Spend two minutes picturing where you want to be in twelve months' time. What creative superpowers do you want to have and how will they manifest themselves in what you are doing? Now open your eyes and draw on the front of the postcard an image of that future.

Step 3 (ten minutes)

---

* Artefact cards are a brilliant tool kit for anyone who works with ideas. The fact that the cards are far more durable than Post-it notes means people are more inclined to craft better ideas on them and they are far easier to collect and reuse. More details on https://artefactshop.com/.

Write down five key things on the back of the postcard that you need to do to achieve your vision. Put a stamp on it and address it to yourself. Then post it.

The couple of days that it takes to arrive back will give your subconscious time to think about those five action points and receiving the postcard will solidify those action points. Put it somewhere where you can see it regularly as a reminder to deliver on those points.

Alternative to the above

Instead of drawing a picture, get a selection of Lego body parts and accessories and build the person you want to be. Use this as inspiration for setting your five key action points.

UNLEASH YOUR BOOM! (TEACHER)
Ten minutes

This exercise is intended to give you a burst of energy when you most need it. All you need is a chair, some quiet space and a pen and paper. If you have never done a visualisation exercise before you might find it difficult at first; if so, we suggest you set yourself a target of doing it twice a week for a month and you will find it will become far easier.

(Please read this very s-l-o-w-l-y first)

Step 1 (five minutes)

Find a comfy chair in a quiet space. Now, close your eyes. Think of a time when you were incredibly creative. You'd just completed a project, piece of art, baked a cake . . . whatever it is, make sure you felt massively proud of it.

Visualise it vividly, smell the smells, hear the sounds, breathe deeply. Touch whatever it was. Hold it up to the sky. Keep visualising it and remembering how you felt. Go deep. Hold that feeling for thirty seconds and then open your eyes.

Step 2 (five minutes)

Now, write down how you feel, what you heard, smelled, touched. Once you have finished writing it down, read what you have written. You should now have a warm glow, a vivid recollection of how powerful you are when you're firing on all cylinders, when you're in the flow. Notice how nothing is a challenge and you feel like you can achieve anything – welcome to your Boom! When you are in your Boom! you are far more receptive to stimulus and creating ideas and you should be ready to unleash your creative superpowers.

BUILDING REFLECTION (TEACHER)
Twenty minutes

This exercise will help you learn from things that happen to you every day. The more you practise it, the more it will become part of your routine and will help you ensure that you are fully learning by doing. All you need is some time and a piece of pen and paper to capture your thoughts. We recommend that you do it once a day for twenty consecutive days to help you build it up as an ongoing habit. It is also worth noting that it may take a little longer than expected the first few times, but it will get quicker as you become more experienced.

Think about a challenging interaction that happened to you when you were in a work or a personal situation and work through Gibbs' reflective cycle, which is constructed as follows:

- **Description:** Describe factually what happened during the situation.
- **Feelings:** What were you thinking and feeling at the time?
- **Evaluation:** List what was good and bad about the experience, or list both the positives and negatives of the experience.
- **Analysis:** What sense can you make out of the situation? What does it mean?
- **Conclusion:** What else could you/they have done? What should you perhaps not have done?
- **Action plan:** If the situation arose again, what would you do differently? How will you adapt your practice in the light of this new understanding?

WHAT WOULD GOOGLE DO? (THIEF)

This exercise is intended simply to make you think differently about a business problem by imagining what someone else would do when faced with that same problem. Again, all you need is time, an open mind and pen and paper.

Simply take your business problem and ask yourself the following questions:

- What would Google do?
- How would Steve Jobs have tackled it?
- What would Michelle Obama do?
- What would Lady Gaga do?
- What would Elon Musk do?
- What would Donald Trump do?
- What would it look like broken down as a set of pieces on the front page of an IKEA instruction manual? What piece is broken?
- How would you draw the problem? Actually draw it. What would it look like if Damian Hirst was drawing it, or Banksy was drawing it?
- What would the betting or the porn industries do (perhaps two of the most innovative industries in the world, driven by the restrictions placed on them)?
- What would the banking or insurance industries do?

SEENAPSE MAPPING – SOFTWARE-ASSISTED INSPIRATION (THIEF)

This exercise is intended to help you open your mind to different stimuli to help solve a creative problem. All you will need is a com-

puter, a registered account (it takes a minute to register) and some time to be inspired.

Seenapse (https://www.seenapse.it/#/whatisthis) is an inspiration engine. It will help you to get more and better ideas faster by providing you with alternative non-linear and non-obvious results which are powered by the mental associations from people all over the world.

You can use Seenapse when you're a bit stuck, or in a hurry, or simply when you want to benefit from diverse ways of looking at the creative problem you're working on. Which, in our experience, is pretty much always.

Using Seenapse is easy: if you are working with something related to, let's say, coffee, just type 'coffee' in the search box. Each of the results can lead you to interesting, divergent stuff that people like you from all over the world have Seenapsed.

The most important thing to keep in mind is this: what you find in Seenapse won't be the solution to your problem, but it will inspire you to come up with it. So don't just look at the Seenapses; go deeper and think about how they relate to the problem, and the solution will pop up in your mind.

Also, whenever you see a Seenapse and think, 'oh, this reminds me of this other thing', go ahead and Seenapse it. In this way you'll be giving back to the other Seenapsers – and when they Seenapse stuff to yours they will help you take your thinking in new directions. Everyone wins.

ALTERNATIVE

If you want further inspiration, you may also want to the creative search engine Yossarian Lives (https://yossarian.co/) which will help you discover new perspectives, conceptual directions, creative insights, and allows collaboration and feedback from a creative global community.

Alternatively, if you find Yossarian Lives or Seenapse too buggy, you could also experiment with a combination of a thesaurus and Google Image search.

GROUP EXERCISES

MASH-UP EXERCISE – PROBLEM SOLVING (HACKER/MAKER)
Twenty-five minutes

This exercise is focused on looking at other innovative businesses and industries to try and inspire you to solve your own problems. It is best in groups of ten or more, although it can be done with as few as four people. You will need:

- Tons of Post-it notes.
- Pens.
- Wall space to stick up the Post-it notes.

Step 1 (three minutes)
Spend three minutes each individually listing as many innovations as possible from the last three years that you have really admired. Ideally, these should come from outside your industry although feel free to include some from within your industry. Write down each on a separate Post-it note.

Step 2 (three minutes)
As a group, stand in front of a wall and in turn share your innovation and then stick it on the left side of the wall. Take one turn each (without repeating any innovation that was shared before) and then repeat until all individual innovations are shared.

Step 3 (two minutes)

Spend two minutes writing down as many problems as you can that you would like to solve within your business (again, on separate Post-it notes).

Step 4 (two minutes)
Again, as a group share these problems on the right-hand side of the wall.

Step 5 (ten minutes)
Now split up into groups of three to five people (depending on the number of people in the group). Each group needs to pick five to ten Post-it notes off the wall from the innovations shared and then pick two to three of the problems you would like to solve. You each have ten minutes to use one of the innovations you admired to solve one of your problems.

Step 6 (five minutes)
Share your ideas as a group with the wider group.

MASH-UP EXERCISE – IDEAS (HACKER/MAKER)
Thirty minutes

This exercise uses the same principles as the previous exercise, but it's focused on creating new ideas rather than solving problems. Again, you will need:

- Tons of post-it notes.
- Pens.

• Wall space to stick up the Post-it notes.

Step 1 (three minutes)

Spend three minutes individually coming up with as many technologies (e.g. VR headsets, AI, mobile phones, wearable tech) as possible. Write each one down on a separate Post-it note.

Step 2 (two minutes)

As a group, stand in front of a wall and in turn share your technology and then stick it on the left-hand side of the wall. Take one turn each (without repeating any technology that was shared before) and then repeat until all individual technologies are shared.

Step 3 (three minutes)

Spend three minutes individually coming up with as many human needs (e.g. food and water, belonging, shelter, entertainment, light, sleep) as possible. Write each one down on a separate Post-it note.

Step 4 (two minutes)

As a group, stand in front of a wall and in turn share your human need and then stick it on the middle of the wall. Take one turn each (without repeating any human need that was shared before) and then repeat until all individual human needs are shared.

Step 5 (three minutes)

Spend three minutes individually coming up with as many services as possible that you use regularly (e.g. Apple Music, Amazon Echo, Deliveroo, Airbnb, Taskrabbit). Write each one down on a separate Post-it note.

Step 6 (two minutes)

As a group, stand in front of a wall and in turn share your services and then stick it on the right-hand side of the wall. Take one turn each (without repeating any service that was shared before) and then repeat until all services are shared.

Step 7 (ten minutes)

Break up into groups (three to five people). Each group should take five to ten Post-it notes off the wall from each category (so will have between fifteen and thirty Post-it notes).

Each team now needs to come up with as many mash-up concepts as possible, a mash-up concept being a new concept which is created by combining two or more things from the wall. For example, if you combine sleep and wearable tech, you get a Fitbit, a device which measures your daily sleep patterns. Or you might combine sleep and mobile phones to produce an app that finds you the nearest hotel that is not fully booked (eight minutes).

After eight minutes, each team should choose their favourite idea and create a catchy name for the concept (two minutes).

Step 8 (five minutes)

Finally, each team is given a minute to present their idea to the whole group, explaining the idea and why they think it would work.

THANKS

Thanks to everyone who continues to support Creative Social as well as our other Utopia communities, namely Brand Social, Innovation Social, and Token Man.

Thanks to all our authors for investing time to contribute your words of wisdom to this book. You are our Creative Superheroes.

Thanks to Kwoky for inspiring the cover and specifically designing our creative superhero logo.

Thanks to Olivier for giving us invaluable feedback on the exercises.

Thanks to all the team at Unbound for supporting us through the whole process and helping make the book as good as it could be.

And, last but by no means least, thanks to all our supporters on Unbound who helped us make this book a reality. We hope you are proud to be in the back of this book.

And hello to Jason Isaacs.

BIOGS

ALISTAIR BARR, FOUNDER, BARR GAZETAS

Alistair's architectural training has led him to champion urban and sustainability innovations. He is a judge for the Academy of Urbanism and Civic Trust and a mentor for the UK Green Building Council's 'Future Leader' programme. His goal is to design spaces where people and the planet can thrive by social interaction.

His creative superhero is Miles Davis, who reinvented jazz many times but whose sound is always recognisable.

Follow him on twitter @barrgazetas

ANNICKEN R. DAY, FOUNDER, CORPORATE SPRING

Annicken is on a mission to inspire work and help businesses thrive in the digital age through focus on communication, leadership and engaged corporate cultures. As former Chief Cultural Officer in Tandberg and Culture Evangelist in Cisco and founder of Corporate Spring, she has inspired and trained thousands of leaders around the world in how to think, work, lead and communicate in the new world of work.

Her creative superhero is Steve Jobs, and two of her favourite quotes are 'Simplicity is the ultimate sophistication' and 'Have the courage to follow your heart and intuition. They somehow already know what you truly want to become. Everything else is secondary.'

Follow her on twitter @annickenday

DANIELE FIANDACA, CO-FOUNDER, CREATIVE SOCIAL AND UTOPIA

Daniele is co-founder of Utopia, a business change consultancy that rewires business for the Age of Creativity. He is also co-founder of Creative Social, a club for creative directors and brand leaders whose purpose is to accelerate creative thinking, and Token Man, an initiative to get men into the gender equality discussion. He is also one of the brains behind The Great British Diversity Experiment. He is also the co-editor and co-author of *Digital Advertising: Past, Present and Future* and *Hacker, Maker, Teacher, Thief: Advertising's Next Generation*.

His creative superhero is Alan Parker, the legendary director of films such as *Angel Heart*, *Bugsy Malone*, *Fame* and *Midnight Express*.

Follow him on twitter @yellif.

DAVID ERIXON, CO-FOUNDER, HYPER ISLAND; HEAD OF DIGITAL & INNOVATION, RBS IN IRELAND

David's key interest is in how people and businesses grow in unstable and converging environments through accommodative learning in strategy, management and culture.

His creative superhero is Camille Paglia, the art historian, writer and cultural critic. Her relentless search for truths about the human condition is infectiously inspirational.

DAVID PEARL (PEARL GROUP), FOUNDER OF STREET WISDOM

David is an innovator in business, the arts and social change. A lifetime performer, he has pioneered the use of arts in the business world. He is the author of *Will There Be Donuts?* and *Story for*

Leaders. In 2015 he invented Street Wisdom, which is now bringing inspiration to thirty countries . . . and counting.

His creative superhero is Stanley Kubrick, a true genius, who was generous enough to give him a pencil and some writing to do.

Follow him on twitter @davidpearlhere

FARIS YAKOB, CO-FOUNDER, GENIUS STEALS

Faris and his wife Rosie have been nomadic creative consultants for brands, agencies, media companies and more, all over the world for the last four years. He is the author of the bestselling *Paid Attention: Innovative Advertising for a Digital World* (Kogan Page, new edition coming in 2018). He created NEW @ LIA awards to champion new kinds of creative ideas.

His creative superhero is Banksy, who made a sculpture of the quote 'Bad Artists Imitate, Great Artists Steal', attributed it to Picasso, then scratched that out and wrote Banksy on top.

Follow him on twitter @faris

HUGH GARRY, DIRECTOR AT STORYTHINGS

Hugh Garry is an award-winning creative thinker, doer, curator and storyteller. Before becoming a director at Storythings Hugh spent fifteen years at the BBC managing creative projects in digital and radio. He runs courses on where ideas come from and with Storythings founder Matt Locke curates a conference called The Story and a storytelling mentoring and masterclass course.

His creative superheroes are Morrissey and Marr because the best ideas are made from elements that shouldn't really belong together, but when connected create magic.

Follow him on twitter @huey

JUSTIN SMITH, FOUNDER, J SMITH ESQUIRE

Justin Smith is a leading British milliner based in London who creates bespoke millinery under the J Smith Esquire brand for a portfolio of private clients. Smith's hats have been exhibited around the world, and have been acquired by such museums as the Fashion Institute of Technology in New York and the Victoria & Albert Museum in London.

Follow him on Instagram @jsmithesquire

KERRY FRIEND, CREATIVE DIRECTOR, BEAR SEASON

Kerry's creative life is constantly evolving. From advertising Executive Creative Director to working with a Civic Tech NGO to a Social Innovation project in the Transkei to curating events-gatherings usually involving using technology to engage and bring people together. So one could say that her career reads as an indistinguishable hacker maker project that's managed to make all the parts work together to keep it going in the same way that a whimsical and mesmerising self perpetuating mechanical nonsense machine does.

Follow her on twitter @kerryfriend

LAURA JORDAN BAMBACH, CREATIVE PARTNER, MR PRESIDENT

A former D&AD President, co-founder of SheSays and currently

Creative Partner at Mr President, Laura Jordan Bambach is a creative force of nature. She is on a mission to use creativity to deliver a better and bolder world and is also one of the brains behind The Great British Diversity Experiment.

Her creative superhero is Patricia Piccinini, who was at the fore-front of 3 graphics when she was at university and has now crossed her work into the real world with a phenomenal humanity.

Follow her on twitter @laurajaybee

LIZI HAMER, REGIONAL CREATIVE DIRECTOR, OCTAGON

Awarded Top 20 Women to watch in Asia, recognised by *Campaign* as a Woman Leading Change across the Creative industry, she's been quoted as having the 'creative enthusiasm of a school bus on the way to the zoo'. Lizi uses her creativity to unite people, tell authentic stories and believes in the power of generous ideas.

Her creative superhero has the truth of Don McCullin, the prolific nature of Andy Warhol and the passion of Lin-Manuel Miranda.

Follow her on twitter @Lizihamer

LUCAS ABELA, MUSICIAN

Lucas is a free-noise musician and participatory sound installation artist whose practice evolved from within the international noise music underground. He is best known for vibrating shards of glass with his mouth to create oddly controlled, while strangely musical, cacophonies performed ecstatically with deft defying techniques.

His creative superhero is Rube Goldberg for making simple things complicated.

MARK EARLS, FOUNDER, HERD CONSULTING

Mark is a pioneering and award-winning writer and consultant on marketing, communications and behaviour change. He has written a number of highly influential books including *Welcome to the Creative Age*, *HERD*, *I'll Have What She's Having* and *Copy, Copy, Copy*.

His creative superhero is David Bowie who repeatedly transformed music and fashion by playing with stuff he found.

Follow him on twitter @herdmeister

MORIHIRO HARANO, CREATIVE DIRECTOR/FOUNDER, MORI INC.

Mori is a multi-talented creative director with stellar achievements not only in advertising but in new business development, strategy, product design and media initiatives. He has had stints at Dentsu, Drill, Party, and founded Mori Inc. in 2012, which was selected as 'The World's Leading Independent Agencies 2014' by *Campaign UK*.

His creative superhero is Sir George Martin, a kingmaker of the most successful commercial entertainment project in history.

Follow him on twitter @I_am_Mori.

NADYA POWELL, CO-FOUNDER, UTOPIA

Nadya is co-founder of Utopia, a business change consultancy that rewires business for the Age of Creativity. She is also co-founder of

Innovation Social, Millennial Mentoring, The Great British Diversity Experiment and the So White Project. She sits on the Executive Committee of the British Interactive Media Association (BIMA), on the Advisory Council of the London Philharmonic Orchestra and is a mum to two opinionated daughters.

Her creative superhero is Salman Rushdie, author of *Midnight's Children* and *The Ground Beneath Her Feet*.

Follow her on @NadsBads

RAVI DESHPANDE, FOUNDER AND CHAIRMAN AT WHYNESS WORLDWIDE

Ravi Deshpande is a prominent creative leader in India and globally. He is founder and chairman of Whyness, an integrated communications agency, as well as co-founder and chairman of Ecole Intuit lab, a French design school. Previously, he helmed Contract India as chairman and CCO, as it won over 600 awards in becoming India's premier creative force. He has been honoured as one of the six living advertising legends of India by the Madras Advertising Club.

His creative superhero is a combination of a film director, a painter, an architect and a cricketer.

ROSIE YAKOB, CO-FOUNDER, GENIUS STEALS

Before co-founding nomadic creative consultancy Genius Steals with Faris, Rosie worked in New York City at Translation, Saatchi & Saatchi, Cake, and 360i helping brands navigate the world of digital. She is passionate about moving the industry forward and speaks at conferences around the world. She believes that brands can create and curate culture, and connect to people in ways that create value for both.

Her creative superhero is Andy Warhol, who embraced brands as a way to comment on and expand pop culture.

Follow her on Instagram @rosieyakob

SCOTT MORRISON, FOUNDER OF THE BOOM!

Scott Morrison is an ex ad man (he ran Nike) and client (he ran Diesel and Levis) turned entrepreneur. He is currently the founder and bringer of the Boom!, helping businesses unblock old thinking, unlock new ideas and unleash their people to make their business go Boom! Learn by doing, make things people want and the cult of done are his mantras. He is also the co-founder of ThinkSprint, a platform for businesses which helps teams problem-solve rapidly by connecting them and their challenges to global experts.

His creative superhero is Maya Angelou, who is always able to touch any heart with deep yet powerful words that we all understand.

Follow him on twitter @scotttheboom

Unbound is the world's first crowdfunding publisher, established in 2011.

We believe that wonderful things can happen when you clear a path for people who share a passion. That's why we've built a platform that brings together readers and authors to crowdfund books they believe in – and give fresh ideas that don't fit the traditional mould the chance they deserve.

This book is in your hands because readers made it possible. Everyone who pledged their support is listed below. Join them by visiting unbound.com and supporting a book today.

Edward Bishop

Jaygo Bloom

Francesca Boardman

James Booth

Rupert Bowater

Barry Brand

Jonny Bravo

Vix Brown

Zena Bruges

Anke Buchta

Andy Buist

Nicola Bullard

Claire Burge

Cordell Burke

Jon Burkhart

Stuart Butler

Colin Byrne

Chantal Cabrol

Jay Caines-Gooby

Lisa Campana

Simon Campbell

Giovanni Canini

Sam Cannon

Liz Carey (Sivell)

Ian Cassidy

Kristy Castleton

Mike Cavers

Monica Chadha

Ashika Chauhan

Hema Chauhan

Susannah Clark

Nick Clement

Aodan Coburn

Will Collin

Paul Collins

Patrick Collister

Brian Cooper

Rob Corradi

Nick Corston

Annamaria Cotroneo

Gemma Cowin

Henry Cowling

Dan Cresta

Anthony Cule

Mike Cunsolo

Sanjai Davé

Terry Davey

Alex Davis

Annicken Day

Gabriella De Matteis

Kim de Ruiter

Ilaria Del Ponte

Dino Demopoulos

Katie Dent Phillipson

Kevin Dersley

Matthew Desmier

Thea Dexter

Sylvia Dick

James Dotchin

Cressida Downing

Franz Drack

Barry Dudley

Kevin Duncan

Ash Durrant

Nick Dutton

Matt Dyke

James Elston

David Erixon

Dirk Eschenbacher

Georgina Estill

Debbi Evans

Tom Evans

Tony Evans

Murray Ewing

Mel Exon
Tolu Farinto
Faris
Tina Fegent
Alexander Fellner
Claire Fennelow
Sonali Fenner
Damian Ferrar
Alfie Fiandaca
Daniele Fiandaca
Ginette Fiandaca
Tina Fiandaca
Ricardo Figueira
Rubens Filho
Kerrie Finch
Graham Fink
Martin Firrell
Daniel Fisher
Fred Flade
Jason Fletcher
Tracey Follows
Amanda Fone
Daniel Fox-Evans
Adam Freeman
Piero Frescobaldi
Warren Frost
Jack Fryer
Helen Fuchs
Hilary Gallo
Patrick Gardner
Jemima Garthwaite
Sarah Gerona
Simon Gill
Soomin Go
Alex Goat
Olivier Goethals
James Goode

Paul Goodison
Beth Gordon
Gav Gordon-Rogers
Emma Grant
John Grant
Sarah Gregersen
Karl Gregory
Matthew Grey
Dafydd Griffiths
Matt Groves
Jo Hagger
Beverly Hall
Lucy Hall
Sophie Hall
Stu Hallybone
Stephen Hampshire
Thea Hamrén
Ali Hanan
Morihiro Harano
Jonathan Harris
Lenna Harris
Pete Harris
Jim Haven
James Haycock
Jon Haywood
Daniel Headey
Andrew Hearse
Bart Heideman
Dagmar Heijmans
Bo Hellberg
Mathias Hellquist
Anna Henriks
Aden Hepburn
John Hiney
Daniel Hirschmann
Adrian Ho
Andy Hobsbawm

Danielle Hoff

Tony Högqvist

Tim Hole

Camilla Honey

Philip Honour

Catherine Hope

Mary Hurlock-Murphy

Sonia Hutton

Mike Imrie

Daniel Jackson

Paula Jago

Erwin Jansen

Vincent Jansen

Alex Jeffries

Graham Jenks

Tim Jones

Ryan Kangisser

Priyanka Kanse

Lins Karnes

Arpit Kaushik

Gareth Kay

Hilary Kemp

Ian Kerrigan

Sulaiman Khan

Dan Kieran

Timothy Klaarenbeek

Hiro Kozaka

Yann Kretz

Candace Kuss

Maria Kwaczynska

Tony Lake

Jonny Lang

Emil Lanne

Alessandra Lariu

Richard Lefevre

Scott Lew

Marc Lewis

Mo Lishomwa

Tamara Lohan

Danny Lucas

Maritna Luger

Gabriela Lungu

Gwydion Lyn

Graham MacInnes

Markus Maczey

Freya Maenhout

Stephen Maher

Danusch Mahmoudi

Anthony Majewski

Maarten Mantje

Jose-Carlos Mariategui

Michelle Marks

Sara Marshall

James Masters

Shib Mathew

Kotaro Matsui

Sophie Maunder

Antony Mayfield

David Mccall

Mel McGinnis

Spencer McHugh

Jane McNeill

David Meikle

Sasha Midgley

Fern Miller

Patrick Mills

John Mitchinson

Katie Moffat

Peter Moody

Soomee Moon

Sam Moqbel

Mark Morley

Casimir Morreau

Deborah Moss

Martin Muir

Bernadette Murdoch

Jane Murison

Jackson Murphy

Lenny Murphy

Carlo Navato

Iain Nealie

Dave Newbold

John Ng

Ana Nicolau

Olivia Nunn

Craig O'Brien

Ryan O'Kane

Yolanda O'Leary

Mark O'Neill

Tim O'Neill

Maryanne O'sullivan

Ian Owen

Danny Pallett

Emily Palmer

Fabio Paracchini

Caroline Paris

David Parkinson

Nicky Parkinson

Mark Passera

Joe Peecock

Emma Perkins

Dan Peters

Peter Petrella

Stephen Phillips

Tim Pointer

Justin Pollard

Edu Pou

Pound & Grain

Matt Powell

Nadya Powell

Iain Preston

Robert Price

Tan Ja Principessa

Roland Pullinger

Purpose-into-action

Gary Pyke

Peter Rattew

Alexander Rea

Emilia Riverstream

Caroline Rixson

Nishma Robb

Tony Roberts

Brian Robertson

Hugh Robertson RPM

Edward Robinson

Richard Robinson

Scott Ex Rodgers

Fernanda Romano

Olivier Rondet

Phillippa Rose

Vikki Ross

Guido Rößling

Seb Royce

Mark Runacus

Leo Ryan

Fani S

Kentaro Saito

Wybe Sallows

Raj Samuel

Andy Sandoz

Dan Saxby

Carol Sayles

Jessica Scharpff

Johannes Schneider

Alasdair Scott

Emma Sexton

Meera Sharath Chandra

Marie Sheel

Sara Silfverberg
Dawn Sillett
Fabio Simoes Pinto
Sveinung Skaalnes
Michael Smith
Davide Sola
Rafa Soto
Ben Southgate
Matt Spry
Marta Stanke
Frisch Stefan
James Stewart
Steve Stokes
Pierre Stokx
Joana-Marie Stolz
Rae Stones
Samuel Tait
Jason Tasker
Renato Tata
Gnome Taylor
Viv Taylor
Mervyn Ten Dam
Mark Terry-Lush
Dan Thwaites
Marc Tobias
Paul Tredwell
Graeme Urwin
Ken Valledy
Craig Vaughton
Joana Veiga
Felix Velarde
Guilherme Vieira
Ollie W
Cary Wakefield
James Wallman
Matthew Watts
Matt Weatherall

Lawrence Weber
Curtis Weir
James Wheeler
Simon White
Gill Whitehead
Elle Whiteley
Zaida Whittington
Gemma Williams
John V Willshire
Belén Wilson
Liz Wilson
Kevin Wittevrongel
Laura Woodroffe
Samantha Yarwood
Matteo Zanaria
Zoha Zoya